# KIN

# KIN

Selected poems, song lyrics
and prose sketches

Barbara Grenfell Fairhead

hands-on books

Publication © Hands-On Books 2022
Text © Barbara Grenfell Fairhead 2022
First published in 2022 by Hands-On Books
www.modjajibooks.co.za

ISBN 978-1-928433-45-3

Editor: Arja Salafranca
Cover artwork: photograph by Jo Ractliffe
Book design and layout: Liz Gowans

Set in Myriad Variable Concept

Printed and bound by Castle Graphics South

For Jacques

## Haiku

In our wedding-bowl
two entwined lovers embrace
the late evening sun


This song that rises
out of you—like clear water
from an ancient well


With each breath we take—
yes!—we are always—always
at the beginning

In acknowledgement of my father

**Pascoe Ernest Grenfell**

RAF squadron leader: 13th Squadron: World War II

You told me to write a book.

And to my six daughters

Jo
Toni
Tamzin
Geordie
Leigh
Trilby

who showed me time and time again—
the magic of innocence.

## THE BLESSING

she made a small crucifix
out of clay
crude
unskilled
artless
but—
from the old Mills cigarette tin
—where she kept it hidden—
he arose to embrace her
and wounded her heart

# EAST GRIQUALAND
*for Barbara and Ege*

Of all the opening lines to the many books I have read, not one calls up more nostalgia for me than Karen Blixen's opening lines in *Out of Africa:* "I had a farm in Africa—"

In my early childhood, I spent many hours drinking in all my father's stories of his youth in Francistown, where he grew up: the trips into the bush and his descriptions of all the animals, their way of camouflaging themselves with stripes, spots and tawny colours that blended in with the grasses. He told me about the dust and thunder of the migrating herds and the deep tracks they left on the ground; the huge elephants and crocodiles in the rivers. All of this was an utterly new world for me. Africa! All the sun and shade, dust and white thorn of it. It was like something out of a precious book.

After the war we came to South Africa as a family of four. Within twelve months my mother, my brother and I were on a coal-driven train on our way to Pietermaritzburg in what was then Natal. We were off to visit her sister and brother-in-law on their farm in East Griqualand.

The train trip alone was an unforgettable experience. The rattle and clackety-clack of the carriages as we moved over the sleepers; the whistle and the billowing smoke; the shouting and shunting at stations, to move onto the correct line—all of this was magic.

And this new landscape. I had never seen so much sun, so much seemingly endless space, as the Karoo offered—a whole day of it. I remember sitting at the train window, leaning on the brass safety bar—drinking in all of it. We only reached De Aar sometime around midnight.

We were met in Pietermaritzburg by my uncle, Ege Pringle. I think my little girl heart fell in love with him, from the moment we met.

We drove between the many green hills, up steep, narrow dirt roads. It was a journey of several hours to the farm, called Dorset, fifteen miles outside Kokstad, and one thousand feet higher in altitude.

My uncle's father first established the farm with his wife sometime in the early nineteen hundreds. They built what was later known as The Old House, close to the kraal and the milking-shed. Beyond the house was the apple orchard.

Ege grew up on the farm, spoke Xhosa before he spoke English, and knew every inch of it like the palm of his hand. He and my aunt built the double-story thatch roof house, about a quarter of a mile from the kraal and higher up the hill, with its view across the lands to Mount May, the neighbouring farm.

We arrived in the late afternoon, just as the mist was rolling down from the mountains, making everything look mysterious.

Barbara, my mother's twin, came out to greet us.

I knew that I had come home.

## PEPPER TREES AT DE AAR
*for Barbara and Ege*

Steam-whistle blowing at the edge of my brain
Smell of Karoo dust after the rain
And a half-remembered childhood coming home from afar
And the tall and always pepper trees
of De Aar

Train-tracks span the plain from day into night
Blood sunset and the cold station light
And a child at the window leaning on the bar
Gazing at those pepper trees
of De Aar

Memories of this landscape printed in my brain
Colours of earth and the rattle of the train
And the sweet smell of evening coming in from afar
And the tall and always pepper trees
of De Aar

## THE GREAT WORK

put aside the great work

comfort the crying infant
the aged dog

put food on the table

go out into the garden
and tend the flowers

if you do this well
it will not be noticed

# HAIKU

Awake in the dark—
I listen to the absence
of a dripping tap—


West wind is blowing—
the white cotton curtains dream
an unfettered sky


This flutter of white—
egrets on the weed-eater—
a halo of birds


A quiet morning—
now see this bright miracle—
washing on a line—

# MATRIX

This year I took a fateful step out of the matrix—
and with the turning of my face
shattered
the remnants of that constricting mould.

I took a step out of the house that has grown me—
that house of orthodoxy
which—however elegant its desire to protect its own—
ultimately destroys us.

I stepped out of that garden with its famous tree—
for no free wind may blow within its high-walled acreage.

And now—I step over that terrifying and beckoning edge
—and fall—
into the dark song of a forgotten woman—
the fierce and sudden heat of her—
and the lonely scent of wild.

I do not have the words for her song—
that ancient longing that murmurs
just beneath the threshold of memory.
But I have the breathing of it.

A sweet breath that breathes me—
pink tongue panting—
animal eyes
—lazy as dreaming—
and slit-lidded against the glare of heat and thorn

a sleek animal—
naked—
female—
with the blood-heat on her—
waiting for the black wind—

# THE RECKONING

My soul
does not want to know what lies beneath this despair—
that there is a place
—older by far than the shining surface of things—
to which an indifferent god
permits us entry.

My soul does not want to know
that all that stands between me and madness
is a thin veil
a mirage
before which I tremble and thirst
and pray
that some saviour without a face
may lift this suffering.

My soul does not want to know
—that should you return to me—
nevertheless
I shall be forever alone.

That should I once again feel your body
in the bed beside me
and your kiss upon my lips
I will know the impermanence of such comfort.

My soul does not want to surrender its love of the body
with all its beauty and the warmth and comfort
of its containment
and certainty

for this painful place—
this hard bright light—
into which I am come.

## NAKED HANDS

Today—
I took off all my rings—

felt the unfamiliar lightness
of hands
—set free—

hands—no longer young—not elegant—

lean—
dexterous—
uncomplicated—

strong hands with bony fingers—unafraid to turn to any task

—and now—

this
strange
nakedness—

# FATHER

What is this startling sorrow, Father
This dark rain?
I feel the wound in my heart
Break open again
Can't hold back this flood of tears
This river of pain
Can't seem to find my way
Back home again

Something is crying me, Father
I can't see its face
Can't hold its sorrow
In my embrace
Can't hold back this flood of tears
This river of pain
Can't seem to find my way
Back home again

What is this wound, Father—this love without a face?
This hidden touch—this dark grace?

Something is crying me, Father
Think they're crying in vain
My footprints lose their way
In the dark night rain
I'm too full of tears Father
Too full of pain
Can't seem to find my way
Back home again

What is this wound Father?
This love without a face?
This hidden touch?
This dark grace?

# EPITAPH

Were you searching for a saviour or an angel
Or a pair of arms to hold you in the night?
Was it love's body that called to you
Like a dark moth burning for the light?

Was that bright desert road too full of questions
And all your prayers too full of night?
Did you long to fly higher than mountains?
Were you drunk on love and longing for the light?

Did you fly too high on fragile wings?
Did you scorch your soul and blind your sight?
Was the earth beneath your feet too heavy
For such a lover of the light?

And when you flew out into space
Did you feel the world turning?
Did you gasp that spirit wind
And taste its burning?

And when you fell to earth
Were you still flying?
Did you catch the wind
At the edge of dying?

## YOU FOUND ME

To know at last this broken song
This sweet ache climbing in the night
This dark earth with its rooted wound
And its hidden light

*Give me your tears and your broken song*
*Your dark kiss to wound me*
*I was alone and lost at the edge of the world*
*And you found me*

To know at last this strange love
This naked touch on the rim of the wound
This trembling shudder as I come to you
Unbound

*Give me your tears and your broken song*
*Your dark kiss to wound me*
*I was alone and lost at the edge of the world*
*And you found me*

# SHE WALKED OUT THE BACK DOOR

It was no sudden decision.

She rose from the kitchen table—

untying her apron
she let it fall to the floor—

kicked off her shoes
and left them
with the worn-down heels and the scuffmarks
to tell their own story.

Barefoot
she walked out the back door.

It was late afternoon.
Underfoot the earth was warm.
She scrunched her toes deep into the gritty sand—
stood with eyes closed—
feeling the masks
and the clothes
and the skins of her past—
fall away.

There would be no going back.

Not ever.

She began to walk.

# GRIEF

This grief
that wraps itself around me
like a woman's shawl
—familiar now with all the contours of betrayal and pain—

or like the night
—tassled with silver and indigo—
—and woven with scatterings of stars—

is like a thing come
at last—

and I—
gazing outward from the rim of night
with death's intimations
made softer now
made sweeter
by this dark night's visitation—

feel a new lightness come to my soul

—like a young girl taken by a lover—

or a dancer
on fire
with madness
and the black wind.

# HAIKU

Stepping out—or—in
it is all one thing—wild wind
still embraces us

# I WANT YOU TO FEEL THE WIND

I want you to feel the wind
Want you to feel the desert wind inside your mind
Want you to feel the empty desert wind
Want you to feel the desert wind inside your mind—inside your mind

I want you to feel that swift cold stream
Want you to feel the backwash tugging at your mind
Feel the reefs and currents streaming through—streaming through
I want you to feel the cold inside your mind—inside your mind

I want you to feel that cold wild sea
I want you to feel it smash into your mind
I want you to hear the thunder of that surf
I want you to hear the thunder in your mind—inside your mind

I want you to feel the wind
I want you to feel the desert wind inside your mind
Want you to feel that cold cruel sea
Want you to feel the cold inside your mind—inside your mind

I want you to feel the wind
I want you to feel the wind inside your mind
Inside your mind—
Inside your mind—

# THE CRAFTING

In this—
our birthing into death
—unlike our first slow shaping—
our souls are rudely struck as if from rock
—a black and bruising ritual of extraction—
and must suffer with open eyes
each blow and spark the chisel serves

—and listen for the ringing in the stone—

as we surrender to that separation
that takes us home.

Could we embrace our fate
with full attention
—and seek not remedy
nor redress
nor intervention—
might we not find ourselves transformed—

our souls miraculously
not broken—
not diminished—
but infinitely expanded by this change—

and our lives
more beautiful—
more authentic—
and more strange—

## DARE I COME INTO TOUCH

*Oh let me touch you*
*Let me hold you in the night*
*Let me taste the sweetness*
*Of this dark dark light*

Oh dare I come into touch
Dare my flesh come alive
Dare I come into your light
Come into your love

Dare I shudder my soul
Dare I know my wound
Dare I come into touch
And let myself be found

Dare I know my passion
Dare I touch that place
Dare I touch those hands
And kiss that face

Dare I know the light
Behind the shadow
Dare I shrive my soul
Of all its sorrow

*Oh, let me touch you*
*Let me hold you in the night*
*Let me taste the sweetness*
*Of this dark dark light*

# A NEW VOICE

To know at last this song
breaking within me
passionate and sacred

and the earth rushing up to meet me
and the dark ibis overhead
sounding his harsh cry
calling out to me to follow

and I
on fire with life's discordant symmetry

—turn my face—

with its old scars
and its new bright edge

—into the uncertainty of that great wheel
—into that hard and fractured light
—into the dark wind.

# NARROW DIRT ROAD

*A narrow dirt road—a blue lagoon*
*The sound of salt—a bent tree—a white stone*

The West Coast is a song
Burns like a fever
A hunger in the mind
Thirsty as a river

The light is a veil
Salt on the wind
The landscape is monotonous
It does strange things to the mind

*A narrow dirt road—blue lagoon—*
*Sound of salt—a bent tree—a white stone*

And I listen to the silence
To the shadow of a stone
To the wide horizon
Empty as a bone

And somewhere beyond my mind
Beyond the chalk road like a dream
I hear the memory of their voices
On the wind stream

I hear the wetlands groan
With the incoming tide
And watch the narrow channels
Grow blue and wide

Dreaming this blue water
This fulling of the tide
And the dark hills holding
On either side

# THAT OTHER WILDERNESS
*for Anna van Esch*
*Jo Toni Tamzin Geordie Leigh Trilby and Kin*

Of her own free will
—and between work commitments—
she entered the eccentric realm of our family life.

Menagerie—
was the only term that could do it justice then
—and some might say even now—
in its contemporary decentralised form.

A rambling house—
the home of six young girls—two parents under a benign siege—
four dogs—four cats—one inherited—two rabbits—
an aviary of budgies—which included—two cockatiels—
and two green parrots.

In addition—
a third cockatiel—in his own large cage—who could whistle
Pop goes the Weasel
—with one flat note on the "pop"—
and—a blue budgie—who
—eventually—
could whistle the same flawed tune.

We rescued a young pigeon called Jake
who
—even when released—
would fly into the house—and peck our heads—demanding to be fed.

To bring this to an end
—and to encourage him to resume his natural life—
grain was sprinkled on the patio.
He did resume his natural life—
and brought the neighbourhood pigeons back with him.
The horses came later.

Our eccentric family life left its mark on her—
like a deep brand.
She became a life member—
and no amount of distance has ever quite erased the mark.


## HAIKU
*for Jo Toni Tamzin Geordie Leigh Trilby—*
*with love—*

Six wild young spirits
—running free in the salt wind—
dreaming blue lagoon—


## HAIKU
*for Kyle, Tash, Zoe, Gus, Chloe, Kayla, Bonnie, Lucas, and Finn*
*Hannah and Noah*

And they did go forth—
and multiply—with some help—
it happens sometimes—

# LAGOON
*for Junie*

I have come here to be alone.
Here—is June Te Water's boathouse, close to the lapping edge of Langebaan Lagoon.
Alone—means that only the small terrier, Tigger, is with me. She is a good companion for this alone time.

We are sitting on the boathouse stoep. This is a construction of seats and flooring, made of large, rough timbers from Sixteen Mile Beach; the washed-up remains, no doubt, of vessels that have been driven by West Coast storms, and the treacherous Benguela current
onto the formidable rocks further north.
This long, long beach
is a joy for any beach-comber, and the inside décor of the boathouse shows evidence of many treasures collected over the years. Only a beach-comber would recognise these as such and would envy the owner. But it is not just a matter of ownership. The large glass balls, which act as floats for the Japanese fishing-nets, can surely be bought. No. It isn't that. It is the finding of them, on a long, wild stretch of empty beach, that makes them precious.
And bones. White, white bones—bleached clean by sun, and salt and wind. Some of these such perfect sculptures, that one can only wonder at the artist's skill.

From where I sit, I look out at a series of low horizontals: the blue lagoon waters; the stretches of sandbars, and islands—all held in place by the low, dark hills.
Even the peace and silence is horizontal.
And the steady, salt wind.

## HAIKU
*for Lindi and her singing bowls*

On another wind
another silent thunder—
held in emptiness


## HAIKU
*for Peta*

And still so present
in your quiet otherness—
I will meet you there

# WEST COAST—DONKERGAT

It is to this place that I return.

It is a harsh place. Because of the combination of sun and an almost constant salt wind, everything that dies quickly corrupts down to its essence. Bones dry and bleach; the blue mussel-shells peel and fade. Carcasses of seabirds, seals, and fish and the long, entangled tubes of kelp, all waste and shrink and curl. The very granite flakes and cracks into brittle shards.

Here time expands, and shadows move slowly around dusty rocks. The light has a clean quality which, together with the glare off the sea, leaches the colour out of the landscape. One becomes aware of light and shadow and the shape and form of things.

Such is the scorching that burns into the land in summer that only the hardiest of plants survive. Many are wizened, and lean close to the ground like contorted bonsai trees, the foliage on the wind-face burnt away. Many of them appear to be dead; but they endure through some inner resource and with the winter rains they resurrect themselves, and send out green shoots and small, vivid flowers.

Many wild animals, for the most part invisible to the casual observer, thrive in this coastal area. I have seen two black-backed jackal at evening-time, crossing an open salt pan, and once I saw a lynx. Colonies of dassies live in the crevices of the large granite boulders, and the sacred ibis can be found the length and breadth of the region.

No trees grow here. Where the animals go in the noonday heat remains a mystery to me. They vanish, and you could be forgiven for thinking the area uninhabited. But if you walk into the scrub, you will discover the many crisscross spoor and animal droppings that testify to their presence.

Here in this stretch of rocky coastline, which marks the end of Sixteen Mile Beach, there is a small, crescent-shaped bay, less than a quarter of a mile across, filled with granite boulders; some egg-shaped, many almost perfect ovals and spheres, the majority far too large to encircle with one's arms.

It is to this place that I return: to allow the wind to wrap itself about me. To listen to the silence and the myriad small sounds of insects shrilling, of wind moving over dry scrub; of dust-devils and waves, and the lost cries of seabirds. To walk the narrow, meandering animal trails. To climb the koppies—to stand where the buck stand and look over the wide sweep of this untamed tract of land to where it blurs into the hazy distance. To feel the wisp of sea-mist floating over my head and melting away as it descends, bringing the barest hint of moisture to my cheek. To breathe in deep breaths of clean air that has travelled over thousands of miles of ocean, bringing with it only the knowledge of space and distance.

It is to this place that I return.

# DONKERGAT

At Donkergat
The whales are still crying
Rattle of harpoon and winch
Sound of whales dying

Sea mist rolling in
South Easter blowing
Dark sounds on the wind
Forgotten blood still flowing

The West Coast sea remembers
Men's voices shouting
Dark shapes in a blood-sea
Flags in the sea mist floating

The pier is black with memory
Green water rising and falling
Smell of blood in the mist
Whales still calling

At Donkergat
The whales are still crying
Rattle of harpoon and winch
Sound of whales dying

# LIGHT
*for Rykie van Reenen
and Jude Wurtzel. Yzerfontein*

Today the sky was full of light.
It filled the eye.

And light was in the water where it rose and fell—
and glancing off the cresting arc of wave—
and in the salt mist that drifted over the land.

The sea was full of foam—
and the waves
—breaking far out—
ran their long rolling whiteness across the bay
to that crescent of sand—
that narrow rim of shore.

And the patient dunes
insubstantial in the whiteness of this light
and the horizontals
softened now
and the gentle contours of the hills.

Today—while you slept—
I lay on your day bed
—my head on the cushion where so often yours has rested—
my face turned seaward
—as yours so often must be turned—
looking out over the bay.

Today—while you slept
—your frail vessel resting in safe harbour—
drawing back its strength from the ocean of sleep
I watched those other boats
returning

from the vastness of
open sea
—fishermen all—
bringing home catches of silver
each small craft surfing in on those smooth swells
through the narrow passage
between Meeurots
and the harbour wall.

Today—as if through your eyes—
I watched the patient sea
lift itself
again and again
over the dark breakwater—

that dark straight wall with its scatter of concrete blocks—
and the sea spilling over that dark straightness
—coursing between those jutting forms—
and the foam
with its whiteness
falling free
falling
over the blackness
back to the heaving sea.

Today the sky was full of light.
It filled the eye.

And I thought—This is your world! This is your sky!
This is the light that so fills you—
so fills your eyes with clarity—
this light that looks through you
its clean radiance—its fearless honesty.

And I thought—
that which you see sees you!

And I thought—
on a day like this—
when the light fills the sky—
and the swelling tide streams over the harbour wall—

and the fishermen come home once more from open sea—
on a day like this—
you will fly out over the bay
—a white gull floating on the wind—

and then—
with that clean light on your wings
—you will make a last wide turn—
—banking into the wind the way gulls do—
a flash of white before you vanish through that blue veil
a spirit wind
filled with light
returning
in the fullness of your odyssey.

## HAIKU

Just the taste of salt—
and the sea mist drifting—and
a full tide rounding

## HAIKU

Within the deepest
silence of stones—the thunder
of an ancient sea

## HAIKU

The deep sleep of stones—
and the mewing of white gulls
over heavy seas

# THE OTHER SIDE OF THE WIND

I can almost see their faces
Floating beyond my mind
Somewhere beyond the sea mist
Just the other side of the wind

Here the painted eland dreams
Footprints across the sky
And the salt-leached light
How it teases the mind's eye

Hear the sound of salt and silence
Of things growing slow
And the rhythm of a rubbing-stone
Against the sea's ebb and flow

There's a white bone taps a taut string
A note that haunts the mind
If you listen you will hear it
Just the other side of the wind

# THE STONES

I am pleased the bay has no name—or if it does, that I have no knowledge of it.

For decades, until it was fenced off some time in the eighties, I used to come to this small bay on the West Coast, with its tumble of smooth, grey stones. There is no other place that I know along this coast that offers anything similar in terms of rock formation.

The stones are all some variation of round and oval—from the smallest, which you can hold in your hand, to others so large that you can lie stretched out on their warm, round bodies. They come at the end of a line of rock that extends across miles of open country and farmland, from the Paarl Rock area.

Does anyone know their full history?

The wind, I am sure, tells stories of how the stones found their shapes, and the sea too, in its own language.

And there are other voices—like the high vibration of sound that I have not heard in other places along this coast: a sound that draws in the silence of shadows and the endless pull of the tides, which might inform us of their secrets—if we could only listen deeply enough.

I know that this area has an ancient history: that this bay must surely have known the footprints of the many peoples who dwelt here so many thousands of years ago.

And, before them—large animals. The presence of fossils of animals, now extinct in this region, tells an even older story.

They have come—and gone—leaving only the barest traces of their passing. And yet, there is something almost palpable in the silence—and I know that I am sharing this experience of wild stillness with them, in a way I cannot explain; cannot begin to understand.

I have spent many hours here on my own in past years, with only gulls for company.

I have felt the wind blow a sea mist over me, baptising me with its sting of salt.

And my own tears.

# HERE IS WHERE

Here is where the deep sea calls the sky—

here is where
the winds divide and meet
and mounting seas hump down
the blunt curve of the long love drown

here is where
dawn's shy light kisses the seven hollows of longing
and blushes into warmth

here is where
the naked manhood of the sky thrusts deep down the narrow green nave
of the sea

here is where
eternal rhythm flows slow
—and high—
—and higher—
till the winds flee before the sweat-warm rain of the sobbing flesh

here is where
—the sky aches—
and lets drop its throbbing fiery orb
into the deep wave wallows

here is where
mood mirrors mood
and sky and sea join
in a great swelling surge and ebb
of warm wet movement

here is where
all is thundering silence
in the sea-shaken skies of sweet pain

here is where
the winds dip and fly in a marriage of time and motion
and fall
in the narrow strip of light
where the cloud thighs part and reveal the bedrock womb of the sea

here is where
thought birds skim
—soft as light—
and soar into invisible sound

here is where
the curling wave holds
—this time—
—and this time—
—and this time—
in a meeting and parting of sky sea sky
rising full
and fuller
and turning
—held still—
for that stroke of time

—which is forever but not forever—
and breaking
in a tumbling sea of light and deep knowing—

and here—
is the rush of free foam up the groaning sands
and the wet sinking slow—

here is the timeless pattern of things.

# REQUIEM FOR A BROKEN WORLD

This is a song of loss and betrayal—
of broken things
and endings.

This is a song of ancestral memories—
of ancient covenants—
and forgetting.

There is a rage in me—
and a sorrow—
and a song of grief so deep and full
my soul suffers the singing.

There is a wound in me that shall not heal—
the deep wound of your kingdom—
the wound of your kind.

In my heart
an elegy—
a song of pain—
a mourning—

in my heart a sorrow
for all wild things—and their passing.

Within me there is an emptiness—pregnant with desire
—to touch
—to taste

     —even the sweat
    —even the blood of your body.

      Within me
   I am pregnant with emptiness.
Breathe one last time your wild breath into me
     —that I may not forget you
     —that I may remember who I am

—breathe one last time your sweet breath into me—

    sing into me your song—
   that it may always sing through me—
   your wild song sound through me—
      forever.

I am singing a song—that has no ending—
    and I shall sing it—
   even as the last print fades—

# A BLUE CORNFLOWER
*for my father:*
*Pascoe Grenfell*
*and his partner in fishing:*
*Leon Roup*

After—
when it was all over—
we came back to this country.

Not the Africa that he loved—
not that place—far north—
the place of his boyhood
that place of red earth and heat—of wide plains and great herds
and nights alone under stars
—the place where he found—and later left his soul
—not to that wilderness where he might have healed himself—
not to that—

but to my mother's town with its suffocating respectability
and its colonial order
and all wildness
—all unruly elements—
contained.
We came back to that.

He was a man unseen
a lonely man
—in exile from himself—
his sadness masked by humour
and a teasing scepticism.

Imprinted in that loneliness
—indelibly etched—
images of death
an untimely shattering of innocence.

But we never heard the stories of the horror and the fear—
only the tales
told and retold
—embellished over the years—
of good times—
of comradeship
of friends with names like Boozlebum and Tanks
and exaggerated accounts of wild sprees across the country
and jaunts to favourite smoky pubs
and well-polished drinking stories.

And sometimes he spoke of his boyhood
—and I heard the poetry in his soul—
the deep response of one who loves wild things
and holds a reverence for their beauty.

But later he spoke less of it.
And finally
not at all.
And what was not spoken
—all the feeling of it—
and the longing for that wild country of his youth
never to be seen again.

But he made a life
—a private life—
—a friend who shared his love of fishing—

the legless beggar outside the store where he bought his fishing-gear
a small dog
—the recipient of his tenderness—
his grandchildren—who worshipped him—
and others.

To these he gave his love—
that huge
shy
embarrassed mix of feeling—
needing
—needing so much—
to find a place for it.

And not all was lost.
A dapper man—he would emerge each day
—from whatever world of night—
—whatever dreams were haunting him—
and walk out into the garden
and pick a blue cornflower for his lapel

—a blue cornflower—
—that deepest shade of blue—

became his badge
a symbol of his courage
—somehow his sign—
that all that wild beauty
that lost life
that love of simple things

—all of this—
still lived somewhere in his heart.



## HAIKU
*My father's koan*

"Why is a chicken
a chicken?—Because it has—
one leg both the same."

# ENTANGLEMENT

So you were not a god
—after all—
father
but a man
and full of human frailty.
I should have known.

And those tangles of fishing-line
that I worked so patiently
unravelling the bird's nest intricacies
of unskilful casts

—those knots still bind my heart—

twisted and complex convolutions
that yet entangle my life with yours—

despite the years
despite your death
despite my protestations.

So that I struggle—and thrash about
like a hooked fish
wounded by desire
and hunger
for some such something
—only glimpsed—

             haunted
       —by a god I cannot name—

for all he reels me in to the new terror of air and shore.

              Reels me in
             —inexorably—

                till I lie
               played out
             a hooked fish
            gaffed and netted

               —at last—

my rainbows gleaming yet from within—
   alive with salt water dreaming—
      beached on solid ground.

# COUNTING THE EMPTY CHAIRS

My father, Squadron Leader P E Grenfell: RAF 13th Squadron, was stationed at a base some distance from London, during World War II.

I have never forgotten listening to his account of what it was like to return to base, after a night's reconnaissance or some active mission. He would climb out of the plane, fill in the logbook, freshen up, and go for a snifter—as he called it—with Tanks, his buddy in crime. Over a glass of whisky, they would share the experiences of the day, muse about how they got lost in dense fog, how the sea, which had been on the right—my father's endearing way of avoiding terms like "east" and "west"—suddenly reappeared on the left.

It has to be remembered that these early planes had few instruments. We may laugh at their simplicity, compared with the swift, sophisticated models of today. Can we ever know the sheer courage it took to climb into one of these 1939 state-of-the-art aeroplanes and fly, by the seat of your pants, almost blind, into dark and dangerous missions?

It was his account of that nightly routine that tells me so much—now that I am older—of what lay behind all his stories: the devil-may-care and bravado, the living as if there was no tomorrow, the jokes about things—too terrifying to feel—in case they overwhelmed the tenuous hold he had on his self-control.

He and Tanks would later proceed to the mess room for the evening meal. In his words, he would tell me what it felt like to walk into that mess room each night—how, when everyone was seated, there would be—one, two or more—empty chairs. How they would all count the chairs—put a name, and a face and a memory to each chair, how no one would say anything; how, in silence, they would keep their thoughts and feelings to themselves.

The chairs, he said, were not removed till the reports came in.

And he spoke about the inescapable awareness that one day it might be his chair that would be empty.

His two younger brothers, George and Arthur, also in the RAF, were both killed in action.

He never spoke about them.

## YOUR EYES
*for Pascoe—my father*

Your eyes speak to me of distance—
of light moving over empty plains
—of silence and shadow—
a certain
intense
quality of listening—

as if your soul
—so attuned after all those years—
could not distinguish itself from that silence.

That soul still is.

Still listens to the silence
of wide horizon—red earth—white thorn—and shadow
—vast open space—
and wild

—still listens to the moon—
to things not visible—
to the fierce blood footprint of wilderness—
and the dark and silent footprints of the night—

still waits—
still listens—
behind the shadows in your eyes—

# THE AFTERWORD

It was probably the last conversation we had.

He had difficulty speaking.

He lay in the hospital bed—
looking away from me.

Not the man I thought I knew
—this almost absent man—
all the light gone out of him.

—And yet—

"You need to write a book—"
he said—

I waited.

"The Diary of a Misfit."

I think it was my inheritance.

# PASCOE'S SONG

There once was a fisherman
Loved by his lonely daughter
Spent his days on an outcast shore
Casting prayers into dark water

*And the fish swim deep and cold*
*Breathing blue water*

A man may spend his whole life
Searching for blue water
Her father was such a man
And she was his only daughter

*And the fish swim deep and cold*
*Breathing blue water*

They say there was a simple man
Walked on blue water
Cast a net to harvest men
Lost like lambs to slaughter

*And the fish swim deep and cold*
*Breathing blue water*

How may a dead man redeem his life
And find that water so blue
Catch the deep and silver dream
A simple man once knew?

*And the fish swim deep and cold*
*Breathing blue water*

Must she stand on that outcast shore
Alone with the wind and the song he taught her—
*Listening—Listening for—*

# REQUIEM

This betrayed kingdom—
this holy season's end—
these desert rivers that find extinction
in a sea of sand.

A febrile wind is blowing over the land—
a lost wind
—empty as waiting—
a dry wind
keening over dust and thorn
drawing out the shadows
and the distance.

And the great herds that imprint their souls
—in the tracery of their migrations—
the rank—the ritual—the blood—the breath—
the unwritten covenant with death—

all this will pass.

*Witness their passing—*
*this final hour—*
*this last slow passage—*
*this migration into silence—*

Last light on Eden—does Eden know this?
Last light on wilderness—on a clean and savage law.
Last light on an order that is older than memory.
Last light on Eden.

*Witness their passing—*
*this final hour—*
*this last slow passage—*
*this migration into silence—*

# LIMPET SHELLS—WEST COAST

You must wait for low tide for the limpet shells.

No. I correct myself. Waiting will only remove you from the moment. Far better to sit on one of the dunes and watch the miniscule changes as they occur to wind and wave.
Small shifts.

This is the training that the eye requires. And all the senses. Not least the ear.

Maybe an hour will pass. Or four. You will not count the time. It is unimportant. You may measure the sea's distance; how it has altered. And the height of the waves. You will detect a new cadence in the wave-sound. Perhaps one might call it sadness.
It is the turning of that tide—a tide which will never come again in quite the same way. It is important to honour this with close attention, to mark its unique and transitory life.

This, too, is part of the training.

Notice how the horizon begins to recede as the waves lose their strength. No more that rush and crash as wave upon wave pushes in—reaching—reaching up the dry sand with its burden of foam and West Coast detritus: a tangled mix of kelp and plastic; rope and pieces of torn fishing-net; the corpses of gull and seal, and full-blown[1] *blaasoppies*.

And strange things to find here: a shoe. An almost perfect orange. And mango pips.

---

1 Blaasoppies: puffer fish

And driftwood. Lovely shapes, worn smooth. You will resist the temptation to gather these. You will not find the delicate rims of limpet shells among this mix.

> Notice how the narrow strip of beach, below the sand dune where you sit, has widened. How the wave patterns, marked by dirty, brown foam, have begun to dry. You might like to walk these patterns—no two ever the same. If you face south, they will take you all of sixteen miles—all the way to Yzerfontein. That might be for another day.
> Do not be drawn into this invitation.

Little by little, the backwash tugs away the heavy, coarse-grained sand. The sea grows small and quiet. Just a soft ripple of sound to the waves that fall, so gently that their tiny rush does nothing to disturb the silk-fine sand; wet sand that, like a mirror, reflects the sky. ☒
You walk up and down this shining stretch of wetness. Training your eye. Training it to respond to only one thing.

And soon the beach will disappear. The blue mussel-shells will vanish.

And all the other shells and sea-offerings.

Time will disappear.

Now there is no you.

There is nothing but the possibility of finding the first rim of a limpet shell.

And this possibility does not exist over and against you.

You are the possibility.

You are the fine rim waiting to be found.

And you are the finding of it.

## SLOWLY—SLOWLY
### *for Jay Louw*

Slowly—slowly
We will do this thing
We will do this thing

Slowly—slowly
We will do this thing

So slowly—slowly
We will do this thing
And love every song that is in it

A song of empty
Desert wind
A call that haunts us

A song of empty
Desert wind
A call that ever haunts us

Song of empty desert wind
A call that haunts us
And memories of things burned clean
Come back to enchant us

*Two survivors—you and I*
*Two lovers of empty places*
*And the beauty of their silence*
*And the always salt-sea wind*

Slowly—slowly
We will do this thing
We will do this thing

So slowly—slowly
We will do this thing
And love every song that is in it

# HAIKU
*for Guy Louw—with a smile*

This untidy tree—
an alien in his eyes—
now—stacked firewood!

# DARK MERCY

I want to remember
The evening light
How it turns blue
Before the night claims it

I want to remember
This faint trace of salt
Still vlei water
And the cobalt that stains it

And the breathing of earth
You standing close to me
And the night reaching out to us
Dark mercy—

I want to remember
These reflections in indigo
Last light
And the slow land that frames it

I want to remember
The hadeda's wild cry
The touch of your hand
Endless and forever sky

And the breathing of earth
You standing close to me
And the night reaching out to us
Dark mercy—
Dark mercy—

## Two White Birds

Two white birds
—in a flash of winter sun—
fly to meet in still waters


## HAIKU

Salt wind and dark vlei—
the drone of the weed-eater—
as I sip my tea.


## Wind Ripples in the Water

Wind ripples in the water—
I catch my breath—
the flying goose has flown—

## HAIKU

*Cold morning—first light—*
*dark reeds pierce the still waters*
*of hermetic night*

## HAIKU

*A broken image*
*—wind-drowned in dark vlei water—*
*shudders up my spine*

## HAIKU

*A sudden night wind*
*—the dark vlei waters shiver—*
*sound of broken moon*

# THE ISLAND

I went to the island today with the dogs—

wind blowing a sheet of white flame off the vlei—
the pungent smell of brak water
frothing in the reeds—

and birds' cries drifting skyward—

fluid light streaming through the flattened wet grass
like a sleek wind in the manes and tails of weather-wild ponies—

and all around a low white sky
—and the pink-tongued dogs running everywhere—

## A DAY GONE

My mother is dying.
She will be ninety-three at the end of this month.

She is slumped—
half-sitting—half-lying in the blue chair.
I sit beside her.
My feelings are like dry leaves
scratching against the windowpane.

She is tiny now—shrunken.
Her skin is like thin rice-paper—
translucent.
Her hands
—crisscrossed with blue veins—
clutch the woollen shawl.
They remind me of a bird's foot.
Perhaps a crow.

She sleeps—
head fallen against the chair's wing—mouth open—
her breathing
so imperceptible
I cannot see any rise or fall.
She will look like this when she is dead.

She does not need to waken for me to see her eyes.
Perhaps they do not look on everyone this way.
Perhaps it is only my seeing draws them so—
as if the iris so contracted the aperture

sharpening the light to a needle
a laser
right through me.

How many years—
the bed—the blue chair—
the chest of drawers—
the small room?

I sit
awkwardly attentive—
searching for the right word—
side-stepping the conflict—
I try to be tender.
I try to smile.

And the dead leaves that have fallen now?
There needs to be a burning.

The rain came today.
It has been a long time coming.
After I left her, I drove up the pass—
sat there with the rain falling—
falling down away from me.

I met my mother today—
held her in my arms—
kissed the faded so familiar face.

We met today—
she is ninety-three years old—
and dying.

The rain has fallen silently all afternoon.
I love her and she is dying.
That is all.

Before this could be written—
she had to die.
Before this could be written—
I had to say goodbye
and allow a part of me to die with her.
Before this could be written—
I had to learn

—that it is the simple things that matter—
and that to discover
after their death
how deeply you love another
—and have been loved—
is to break your heart.

# WINTER

Winter—the tides of grey
that sweep over the land
remove all colour and definition
—leaving only ghosts of mountains and trees—
and a flatness where I stand.

Between the squalls
the light is hard and bright
winter sun against a black sky
etches such clarity
into tree-branches—the texture of bark
and the streaming grass—wet and wind-torn.

There is a turning happens now.

Everything submits to the season—
slows down—
brings its energy into itself—
to sleep—
to remember.

A time of quiet introspection.

My mother died a year ago—
we cast her ashes on that mountainside—
hidden now
in rain.

Today I remember her—
recall that day—
that hour—
the last crossing she made.

# WILD BIRD

Wild bird
from a dark sky
in the saltmarsh
—waiting—
casting across the mudflats
—your longing cry—

and lonely the wide reaches
—with only the wind to hear you—
calling
for the mate
who is gone.

# HERON

There is the slow march of a heron stilting through the reeds
and a settle of birds on quiet waters
—and beyond—
the dark shadows of the wind.

A round tide is fulling
and a night wind breathing
and a red sun dying in a patterned sky
—all as rhythmic as the contours in the ploughed ochre lands
and the stubble fields bleaching.

And high—
and clear—
and pure—
one sweet voice chanting
a simple earthy faith—

"Oh, I would fold thee in my loving arms
and warm thee with my kisses—Jesu."

And even the drunken scarecrow
finds his own belonging.

Why then
—in all this quiet wholeness—
am I so strange?

# KIRSTEN'S SONG

*In memory of Kirsten Guy Louw*
*for Guy and Jay Louw*

I hear a deeper call
Sounding down the wind
Within the beating of my heart
Beyond the shadows of my mind

I hear a deeper call
A song of beauty in my brain
An ancient covenant within me
Calling me home again

And I must fly this swift migration
While the song sings through me
A song of wild places
Calling to me

I hear a deeper call
Sounding down the wind
Within the beating of my heart
Beyond the shadows of my mind

I hear a deeper call
A song of beauty in my brain
An ancient covenant within me
Calling me home—

## FALSE BAY COASTAL ROAD
*for Julian Roup, Xanthus and Malarky*

Sand sifts across the potholed tar.

A narrow stretch of beach
—a sinuous ribbon of sand—strewn with dark shapes—
kelp—lumps of red bait—colonies of gulls—
separates road from sea.

Sometimes
—a fisherman makes a lonely vertical against the low horizon—
but more often the coastline is deserted.

Low hills float on the sea mist
—insubstantial as dreams—
or clouds and rain close in the world
to a bowl of whiteness
around me.

An unforgiving salt wind blows the light across a choppy ocean
—to fret itself against the sandstone cliffs—
that lean out over the sea.

And overhead
—gulls float and slide across the sky—
random as scraps of paper in the wind.

The road cuts a dark line through the white-dune coastland—
then slips its way into a landscape of salt-burnt vegetation.

The speeding verge blurs into sameness.

The only intrusion
is the hypnotic
—flick-flick-flick—
of the staccato white line
that races by me

—urgent as a leaping hare
caught in a beam of light.

# TOTEM

A square blind shack of corrugated rust and iron—
a cube of metal
—a blank die the colour of dry blood—
stands alone on the dune.

No windows
mark the weathered flanks.
No door.

It stands
—a solitary—
at the very edge
of a wind-blown and broken shore.

Behind it
a vast and blinding ocean of iron
—shimmers with heat—
and stretches wide its vast sprawl—
staked and pinned to the low-lying undulating flats
like some totemic animal hide
strung out
—taut and nervous—
across the melt of countryside.

And all around
denuded slopes stare their blind unlidded stare
and the unremitting wind
blows the white sand bare.

Someone has set two pairs of kudu horns
where roof meets wall
—dark horns—
that spiral up defiantly to pierce the sky—

—and the blood and rust flanks—
—pant and fall—
and a blind and corrugated face outstares it all.

What proud spirit of Africa stands here—facing east?

What creature is it stands here
—bleeding dry rust—
stands alone
—dark and raw and skinned?
What powerful totem is it
—leans its will—
into the driving wind?

# THE ROAD HEADS EAST

The road heads east—
casting its thin ribbon of tar over coastal hills—
skirting the windswept wastes that run parallel to the sea—
a fine black line that travels over desolate topography—
etching into memory the longing for mountains.

This road has become for me a place of no dimension—
—a threshold between two worlds—
—where the two worlds in me—
meet
and find separation.

There is a point where the road
turns—
and leaves the sea behind—
turns—
the way a salmon turns to face the current
turns—
to swim against the river's flow
turns—
and heads upstream
seeking clean
cold
mountain water.

And always there comes a moment
—an instant—
some kind of crossing in my mind

and this astonishing excitement
—this leaping of the blood—
that says—

"Yes!"

And then I know that I too have turned—
that I too have left the sea behind me—

and I am on a new river
—old as dreaming—
and heading upstream—
breathless—

seeking a new dream—
seeking the origin of dreams—
seeking my own source—

# MISCHKA

Something of stillness
of space
of silence
something of the memory
of frozen landscape
lies etched
within
that Arctic gaze.

In the twin pools of her eyes
the pale blue
reflections
of a northern sky
are pierced with black.

No disquiet
shadows the clarity
of that intense stare.

Her eyes meet mine
directly
to ascertain my rank.

Far from her origins
those cold and silent wastes
the authority of her ancestry
remains.

May I never tame her—

only find that simple place
where I let slip my fetters
and meet her in the memory
of that uncorrupted land.

# YOUR FACE

Your face
Your bright face
Day and night is all I see
This face
This lovely face
This haunting gaze
Haunting me

How I love your strangeness
The otherness of you
And your unbroken shadow
Running free
And your stillness
And your wild heart
Fierce love
Breathing me

In forest shadows
Deep in the heart of me
I hold the image of you
In my memory
And your bright face
And your pale blue eyes
You—always you
Running back to me

Your face
Your bright face
Day and night is all I see

This face
This lovely face
This haunting gaze
Haunting me—
This haunting gaze—

# THE HEART OF THE HOUSE

They are possibly the last two guardians
of such unique
and individual loyalty—
that I will know in my lifetime—

a Beagle and a Labrador—
the first—a farce—indeed
—and to be reckoned with—
the second—a guide dog
of generous heart.

Who else but a lover of dogs
can ever know
—with what humility—
the depth of their unconditional love—
the healing gift of their silent communion?

## HAIKU
*for Digby*

*With senses alert*
*—guardian of his domain—*
*indomitable.*


## HAIKU
*for Cracker*

*In this scattered world*
*the doggedness of his love*
*holds us together*

## REQUIEM FOR A BELOVED

Fold her in gently
into your dark earth
into the compassion
of your mysterious silence.

Root and rootling
—craft for her a caul—
to safeguard her soul
on the dark night sea.

The light has gone—
and her patient courage sleeps
and the gathering of her days
—is consummated now—
in death.

Watch over this sweet soul
unbound at last.

# FREYJA

First light
half sleep
—where many worlds play—
a sensual breath is breathing me.

In this place
—where all things pass—

I breathe in deeply
the sweet one breathing me.

# FRITH

The light has gone now.
I shall not see her again.

No argument can comprehend such finality
when the absence of her is everywhere.
Memory will not permit this departure
nor my soul accept its loss.

The light has gone

—and all those places that she loved—
those quiet places—so intimately hers—
are empty now
and filled with the imprint of her character.

Something broken now—so painfully lost.

Something
—some way of being—
no longer simple.

The light has gone.
How can it not be here?

What draws me down into this dark place?
Who is the child calling in the night?

From what manner of god
is such light given
to cast such shadow?


## HAIKU

Death has closed those eyes.
To what country does the soul
fly—when such light dies?

## FOR THE DEAD ONES

Where are you now
with your lovely light
and your clear voices
that still echo in my brain?

If I close my eyes
I can still see you
in the dappled light
of a quiet forest.

And—
should I step through that mysterious veil—
surrender myself to that unknown god—

shall I find you again
and touch your faces?

Shall I be with you once more
in that timeless land?

## HAIKU

Such unfailing love!
Where did they learn it—you ask?
They didn't learn it—

# THE BONES

We had to disinter them—move them to another place.

I did not want to look
—afraid of that taboo—
afraid to cross that line
afraid to see
—to know too much—
and then
—out it fell.

It just fell out
—that one long yellow bone—
fell out from the others when we laid the bundle down
this long—this yellow bone—
lay there
—naked on the earth—
alone.

It fell only a little way
and lay there
smooth and yellow in the pit—
and I
—so not to spoil her sleep—
just barely touched it
edged it back
beneath the coverlet.

She lies there now
sound in earth and loam—
a tree to mark the place—and that one large stone
—hidden—
returned to silence—
and the long forgetting night
folding her in—

But that bone—that just fell out—
that yellow bone—I did not want to see

—that I have touched—

refuses to die—
refuses to be unseen—

it speaks to me—from that dark and hidden pit

—confronts my memory—
as if to say—

"You know only the part of it—"

# COURTYARD

In the small courtyard where I sit
the tamarisk wears tendrils of pink
and a blur of summer bees.

Hadedas sound their strident cries
and fly low over the trees
to the wetlands.

And the waterways
lie still.

In the small courtyard
where the tamarisk casts
a lacy shade on the pink-powdered bricks
and the sea wind sighs through the salty pines—
the world breathes its wild nature song—
barely tamed by my contrivances
and the containing walls.

How many times do I walk through this world—
not hearing its urgent voice
that reminds me who I am?

And all the while
the orchestra of life
—full of blood and spirit—
of sap rising
rain falling
of passion

death and fury
—is sounding its earth-cry—
—its raw note—
—calling me—
to surrender myself into the mystery of things—

## A ROSE IS NOT A ROSE
*—with apologies to Gertrude Stein*
*for Stephen Watson*

A rose is not
a rose
is not
a rose
—but a becoming—

an energetic rise and swell of sap
—a seminal and saturate solution—
to nourish every stem and leaf
and node
—and every wounding thorn—
drawn upward by the absence
of the bloom.

And so—
to the advent of the bud
small
tight
waxy
—and full of waiting—
gathering all the parts of generation—
stamen—carpel—pistil—petals—the lot.

And finally
the parting of the sepals—
and the breathless unfolding
of each concentric whorl

  —petal by sensuous petal—
  into full-blown fragrant presence
    unfurled
  —the naked revelation of the rose.

   And no less lovely
  the sigh of each slow petal's falling—
and the new-formed sanctuary of the woody pod
  closing upon the silence of the seed.

  This is the law and legend of the rose.

# REFLECTIONS ON AN OLD TABLE

It was waiting for me in a small shop
—an old pine table—
covered in dust and grime
and bric-a-brac of no single ancestry—
not an elegant piece
but sturdy-legged—of kitchen mode
that had not begged nor complained
—in over a hundred years—
its lot or its load.

The rivers of Oregon
still flow through the worked timbers—
and the winds intrinsic to that place of origin
—still blow a stream of memory through the hard and golden grain—
still remember great stands of trees
fed by mountain mist
and silence
and rain.

The patterns that inform its woody soul
are sinuous maps of its beginnings
—echoes of the whole—
of a great river journey
of currents and eddies
that carried the mighty trunk of tree
a journey of long slow years—and long slow weathering
downstream to the sea.

I have cleaned away the dust and grime.
It is functional.

A white enamel billycan of silk poppies
and a wooden duck called Emilio
—carved and fixed in time—
and a fruit bowl
now grace its surface.

Emilio stands
—throat stretched out and full of soul—
and gazes up his wooden stare
at the bright and multi-coloured aureole.

Each day I come with beeswax polish
and work my soul into the mat surface.
With waxy fingers
I trace
the river lines
mainstream
and arteriole.

I will do this again and again
until
—one morning—
I shall enter the room
—and find—

Emilio
—gazing in astonishment at another of his kind—
gazing in wonder at his reflection—
the graceful sinuous curve of neck inclined—

his eye bright with recollection—
and his face
—in that shining patina—
a clean image
mirrored to perfection

—a face radiant with delight—
floating in a river of poppies—
pink and yellow and scarlet—and white.

# PRUNES

There is so much you can do with a prune.

Of course—
some say
better to eat the plum freshly plucked.
But I could argue that.

A plump prune—
full and sweet with summer sun—
its textured flesh
—lost and luscious—
made darker by a certain weathering
—and voluptuously delicious—
so that it lingers on the breath
long after it is eaten

—well now—
that is something!

And then
of course
—those wanton prunes—
wide open for the taking
and filled with just the right amount
of creamed white cheese.
Ah—how they kiss the palate.

And prunes—roasted soft
and wrapped around with long thin bacon reins

—"Devils on Horseback" I think they are called—
sweet and salty as any sweat-drenched kiss—
a must for any prune connoisseur.

There are prunes that lie soft inside baked apples
—dreaming of Eden—
and others that stew and bubble dark their syrup
—wild as wanting—
till the flesh falls from the silent stone
and cleaves like manna to the tongue.

You find prunes everywhere—
de-pipped
spun into nectar
fit for any god.

Oh yes!

Even the gods acclaim
such swarthy—purple—sweet—full-breasted succulence.

And then—
there is that small unfortunate—
the ungenerous prune.

The prune not offered—
not taken—
not tasted—

but left to lie—
small
and hard

and wizened
in the bowl.

She has no virtue
though she may deceive herself in this.

She lies
shrunken by respectability
in a bed of tedious wrinkles
clasping in skin-thin desiccated hands
the lonely
    stone
    of her
    heart.

Her summer passes

like a dream not dreamed.

It will not come round again.

How could she not know this?

# LATE SUMMER

I came upon late summer
—blowing—
in the corner of a far-flung field
and marvelled that such fierce sun yet burned in its embrace.

A wild tangle of uncut grass
and flowers
—sweet for their lateness—
surrendered their will to the lazy wind
offered their sweetness to the day.

In such a flame
—in such desire—
what could they know
of winter?

This poem then—
a seed
I place in loamy earth
and touch with naked hands and fingers
—innocent of all design—
that unseen place of silence.

I make a small hollow
—shape it to my palm—
and lay the tiny blueprint
—of all that I hold holy—
into its dark keeping.

# COVENANT

I have met him
in remote places
always close to the edge
of that breaking line.

For the briefest moment
he shows himself,
then, sensing an intimacy
that will compromise his solitude,
instantly
is gone.

I have met him
in remote places,
always alone.

There is a wounding in his eyes,
a despair impossible to hide,
as if, through some extreme initiation
his young boyhood was stripped
too naked:

some trust—
that deep illusion that subdues
our childhood pain—
broken too soon.

The gods abandoned him.
An older law
was his inheritance.

Now in remote places
I hear the stark notes
of his song,
his covenant
with a world that breathes
beyond all written law—

enduring—
strong—

## HERE I AM
*for Danie*

Here I am in this moment

—in a world of gentle rain and grey—

and I have fallen in love
with that sweet
ineffable sadness

—which whispers to me—

above the noisy din
of this every day—

## HAIKU

This most precious thing—
so close—how could you lose it—
how could you hold it?

## HAIKU

One small candle—lit
and all darkness in the world—
must bow before it.

## I Know Now

I know now—
as I have not known before—
that the world will not own me—

# GREY

No wind—no mountain

—soft rain falling from a grey sky—

and the tall bottle brush in the courtyard

—weeping—
slow red tears.

Only the sunbirds
remember summer.

# ENDINGS

A long summer we had this year—
a summer—it would seem
—reluctant to make her bow—
as if—at the end
—only when the last late blooms began to fade—
only then
did she know her beauty.

Something about these days
—something—not quite definable—
but felt
in some inexplicable way—foreseen
—longed for.

Something—
almost lonely.

Something about the lazy falling leaves—
the late sun sloping thinly down the hills—
the bent and naked torsos of the vines—
the chill of evening—falling early now—
a quiet withdrawal into night.

At times like these one knows
the certainty of endings.

When I return to the forgiving earth
a small bundle
scarcely more than bones

from time to time remembered
—the way one recalls a day from childhood—
or perhaps
a fragment of a poem we once heard—
will I still have with me the memory of my song?

I want to be buried in open ground—
or have my ashes cast over West Coast land—
have some wild creature
tread me deep
into that sand and loam—
I want to return as rock
or salt
or wind.

Place no mark or stone where I am laid—
I want the comfort of anonymity and forgetting.

Already I have knowledge of earth and night
—and the great silence that enfolds one like a shroud—

I want no last rites
no prayers
no sad tears

only the evening light
to fall gently upon the place where I am laid

and
finally—

to know
the merciful compassion
of night.

# TOKAI

My heart fills
with the sound of rain
and the forest
rattling its bones
in the storm—

and I remember
that wild afternoon—
and the dogs
—mad with excitement—
and me with fear
of lightning
and branches falling—

and still we made the whole circuit
of the wild wet wood—
filling ourselves with the rage of it—

# WEST COAST ROAD

It was on the way back that we saw her.

All around, evening was falling. Mountains floated on the valley mist, and a dying sun lit the purply sky. Tufts of dry wheat-stalks etched the corners of the ploughed lands, and soft, wide space was everywhere.

I could picture her in that last light—every whisker alert, ears back, straining to detect the slightest sound; soft, wet nose quivering with the scents of approaching night.

I have followed each frame of that wild, fluid run, over and over in my mind: have watched that leaping flash of tawny and white, as she raced toward her end.

Could I replay it just one more time, and change by an instant her destiny?

For there was that last leap with all her wildness in it—one last leap that took her far from these brown plains, past the distant, purple mountains, into the dissolution of time.

Did she see what sped her to her end, as her body arced this world and another? In that snatch of time, which is no time at all, did she feel a distance from the noise, the impact and that flying form? And did she look back at the tawny body lying motionless on the road, and feel a connection with the still form, the soft, white throat, the dark-tipped ears?

Or was it all too quick? Did that instant erase all sense of separation?

Was the moment of death an exultant awakening—and was this, the greatest of all crossings, a passage of ecstasy?

All we saw was the dead hare on the road, her body still—stretched out in that last leap—with the blood drying now around her nose and mouth.

That is what we saw as we hurtled past.

# THE DUNES

It can take a lifetime to attune your ear to the soundless voice of the desert dunes; to hear that centuries-slow yawn of time sounding its deep and silent note.

And even then, you can't be sure of those vast, inscrutable entities whose faces shift endlessly as they sculpt themselves against the wind.

You can spend a lifetime listening, yet never come to know the full truth of them—for even as you gain some measure of familiarity with just one of those countless millions, it will recede, taking its secrets with it in its slow migration across the landscape.

I am drawn to dunes, drawn to the clean edge of their beauty; drawn to that certain place where a clean-cut line becomes a smooth body of form, a gentle rounding. Drawn to the dramatic effects of light and shadow on their concave slip faces, which form below the crest, and to the textures of the convex planes.

I am fascinated by this transition—how it is impossible to say: here—this is where the change occurs.

I observe how a sharp edge, a line separating light and almost black shadow, becomes a plane where the change happens grain by grain, shaped by wind with such subtlety that I cannot see just where the shift occurs.

I am in love with this indefinable place, which refuses to let itself be known, in love with the grandeur of these shifting forms, in the presence of which I am nothing.

Yet, I am not prepared to venture alone into their hypnotic landscape with its endless repetitions.

They would show no mercy to an intruder. Of that I am certain.

But here where I am sitting, further south, these small coastal dunes with their tufts of wispy marram grass and small succulent bushes, these low, white dunes that separate Langebaan Lagoon from the sixteen-mile-long stretch of coast between Donkergat and Yzerfontein are hospitable. They will allow you liberties that the Namibian dunes will not forgive.

I have come here to be alone.

I am sitting on a white dune facing the sea. It is the afternoon of my last day here—alone. Almost alone. The small dog is with me.

We have been sitting here for hours now. Doing nothing. She is old enough to enjoy this.

She is sitting in the shade of a small bush, panting her pink tongue towards the sea. She sits with eyes squinting against the glare of the white sand. From time to time she shifts her gaze, and I see her nostrils quiver with some fresh scent carried on the wind.

Behind us, out of sight now, lies the long, wide stretch of blue water. Langebaan Lagoon. We have spent our nights in a boathouse, maybe fifty yards from its shore, listening to the wind and the lapping of the small waves.

On our second night, a wind out of the east—the taut lines of nylon that are stretched over the roof vibrate with an eerie sound, an ancient lament. Not quite human. I have been told that it comes from the voices of the

Strandlopers who used to roam these parts. All gone now.

In front of me there is a small hump of sand, which has formed around a bush. Above this there is a bed of tough, sleek marram grass through which the wind streams, tossing the bending grasses this way and that like the manes of wild ponies.

Below these, the small bush clings to the sand. I notice that some of its roots are exposed, and that on the wind-face a salt wind has burnt away the foliage. One broken, twig-like branch hangs down over the gentle slope.

Each gust of wind etches a line—a faint line of shadow—onto the white sand; onto a complex pattern of lines, no two ever exactly the same. These wind-etched lines endlessly overwrite the previous pattern. The result is an ever-changing composition, an arc of delicate design—barely half a circle's worth. This is the extent of the dead twig's reach. It is an image as fine and elegant as a Japanese artwork.

I have been watching it for over an hour, partly mesmerised by the subtle variations, fascinated by this visible effect of an invisible force. And soon, the wind from some other direction will erase it, leaving only the blank stare of the white sand. I appreciate that part of its beauty lies precisely in the transitory nature of its appearance.

Beside me I have placed a small pile of pink snail shells. These I have gathered on our walk across the wide back of the dunes, stopping each time we come to a place where they lie, scattered below the patches of vegetation. I have never found any of the live snails. They obviously live here, but how they survive the build-up of salt is a mystery to me.

Now I pick up one shell and examine it. I marvel at the perfection of the spiral, which increases with a mathematical precision as it moves from the apex to the mouth. I notice that the growth has not been even, that there are variations in colour and texture. I draw my nail over the shell and feel ridges, which are more pronounced in places, telling something of the snail's life passage.

I pick up a second shell. To the casual observer it is the same as the first. But look! How different the shades of colour and texture. And one raised ridge that speaks of some snail trauma during its lifetime.

It is filled with sand. I tap it. Nothing happens. With my finger I scratch the sand at the mouth of the shell. I tap again. A little sand falls out. The weight of the shell, and its dark, pink colour, show me that it is filled with sand, right into the narrowest part of the spiral. I need a tool to loosen the salt-caked opening; to allow the inner sand to run free.

I get up and walk about, looking for a dry twig. The dog runs up and barks, pleased to be on the move again. I find my twig and return to the place beside the shells. The dog returns to her position in the shade.

If a mantra could be translated into an action, it would be this—this cleaning of the pink snail shells. It is a delicate operation. Scratch out as much sand as you can with the twig. Hold the snail shell so that the opening faces downwards. Tap gently. A little sand falls out. Repeat this scratch and tap several times. Each time a little more sand falls out.

I now see that it helps to turn the shell as I tap, so that all the sand caught in the tip of the spiral can move its way through the hidden passage. With the last tap, all the remainder of the sand is released. I notice that this is dark, almost black. I presume this to be the remains of the snail, which have been cured and dried by salt and wind.

I hold in my hand the clean shell. I turn it over. I look into the mouth—the opening with its thin lip. Here the pink is far darker, almost lilac in colour. It has a nacreous shine which reaches deep into the shell, offering a smooth inner surface.

It is the sudden change in temperature that brings me back to the day. A sea mist is beginning to drift over the dunes. It has almost blotted out the low sun.

I gather up my pile of shells and put them into my collection bag, where they rattle with the sound of old bones.

## WELWITSCHIA MIRABILIS

Let me speak to you of solitude
—this I know.
And silence.

And of time counted in centuries—
and the imperceptible patterns of my silent growth.

Time
—so enduring in its endless repetitions—
that it merges
into timelessness.

I know what it means to live with emptiness—
to arrive at a place
beyond hope—and hopelessness.

To be content with things so small
they challenge measurement itself.

I stand rooted in scorching sands
my head
—floating in the mirage—
my gaze embracing heaven—

by day
—only blue from horizon to horizon—
by night—the stars—infinity.

I have forgotten what is meant by patience
—although I do remember the word—

this too does not concern me
nor any manner of self-reflection.

I know only that I am—
and of death—
that it has its season.

## HAIKU
*for Laurence Platt*

What is emptiness?
Let me see your other hand!
Which other hand? — Yes!



## HAIKU

What is this nothing—
this no-thing—yet every-thing?
No one can tell you—



## HAIKU

What is the time—now?
Only a fool would answer—
But who would ask it?

# CAPE FRIO SEALS

No mercy in the wind
Sea-fog and the hush of waves
Desert behind me—vast and silent
Skeletons of memory and the Cape Frio seals

I am broken to the bone by this desolation
I am broken to the bone by the beauty of this land

An empty land in a shroud of mist
Skeletons of ships and whales
Untamed water and the sound of waves
And the sudden presence of the Cape Frio seals

I am broken to the bone by this desolation
I am broken to the bone by the beauty of this land

# THE BREEDING SEASON

The breeding season was over, and most of the seals had departed from that long, desolate shore.

The small colonies that remained were scattered at intervals along the shore—dark, irregular lines in that colourless stretch of nothing. A sea mist drifted in over the land, blotting out all distinction, removing all perspective and distance, muffling the sound of wind and wave.

As we came close to them their heads turned and, seeing the dark form approaching, they rose, humped and flapped their ungainly way down to the cold, green waves.

There were others that remained on the beach when we passed. They were not in groups, but lay alone, facing the land—old, thin seals, their bones clearly visible under their dull-brown fur. They turned their heads at the sound of the engine, and some tried to rise, but their old bodies could no longer respond. Only their eyes watched as we went by.

One or two had a last young pup, waiting persistently nearby. They too, perhaps unknowingly, were summoning their death. They skipped into the sea as we passed; but looking back we saw them return to the land, to the familiar form, unable perhaps to break the invisible cord that held them there.

It was dusk when we passed the last old seal. I saw her eyes quite clearly as she turned.

I have this thing about an animal's eyes—a fascination, a haunting maybe, some truth there that my mind cannot hold, cannot conceptualise in any way. I feel, somewhere in my gut, the voices of these and other eyes that meet mine—on township roads; behind wire; in cages; and here on this wild stretch of coast: we speak across some rift, some split that was invented—how long ago?

# SKELETON COAST: THIS DESOLATION

This desolation
Fills a longing inside of me—
This narrow edge of nothing—
This wild sea—

Crashing of the waves—
Crying of the gulls—
This naked wind
Inside my skull—

Inside my skull—

Beauty and death
Inside my skull

Crashing of the waves

Crying—

Crying—

# FOLLOWING THE RIVER—SKELETON COAST

We have been driving in the Land Rover for over an hour.

We are following the path of a dry riverbed as it travels towards the sea.

As we drive on its smooth, white-sand surface, we notice the tangle of vegetation on either side, which speaks of hidden water.

Finally, we arrive at a place where the riverbed narrows to pass between two sections of brown rock.
We have to cling onto the vehicle's frame, as it literally climbs through and down this narrow, rocky gorge.

A little way on from this we stop and cut the engine.

The sand is darker here. It is moist.

We are told that the river is still flowing, beneath the surface.

We sit quietly, watching some springbok that have come, searching for water.

## HAIKU

Desert antelope
walk the dry wide riverbed
drinking their footprints

## I Grieve these Desert Rivers

I grieve these desert rivers
that find extinction
in a sea of sand

# ABSENCE

An absence haunts the land
Like a forgotten dream
An unwritten story
In a salt slipstream

Footprints on the wind
A shard of burnt clay in the hand
A painting on a rock
An absence in the land

Memories of a people
Written on the wind
Footprints in the landscape
Haunt the mind

Footprints on the wind
A shard of burnt clay in the hand
A painting on a rock
An absence in the land

An absence in the land—

An absence in the land—

# KUNENE RIVER

This is a land surrounded by silence
Naked as a bone
A land of brutal beauty
Wind-blown

A ribbon of sudden green
Red sand
Kunene River
Desert land

# IMPRINT

In the cutting
coarse white sand glistens like frost
and the tall dark trees
stand like gods
etched in stillness
breathing in the after-rain sky.

I am not alone.

At my feet
incised into wet earth
—a paw-print—
freshly made.

Four claws and the deep impression of the pad
—a clean-cut character—
in the wet
white sand.

I do not have his story—

only that he travelled swiftly—
that much I can tell—
and that there was passion in it.

He left nothing that could be possessed
—only his mark—
the momentary imprint of his passing.

And he had no mind to leave even that.
To be remembered was not his intent.
Only—
that his spirit raced ahead of him
—and the pumping blood
—and the warm fur and flesh of his soul
—leapt out to follow.
He left behind an absence in the forest.
An emptiness where he had been.

Four clean claws in the wet white sand
—and the round full firmness of the pad

—an imprint incised into wet earth
—an image imprinted in my brain.

# ALONE
*for Thello*

What was it that flashed between them—
the solitary woman—and the ageing wolf?

There were others there—as well.
But this is not their story.
This is a story of Alone.

This is a story—
an instant of recognition—across a great divide—
across an emptiness—so vast—it is immeasurable
yet will admit all difference—
so long—
so long as true presence presides.

There are images from this time—so many of them—they fill the mind.

Yet—there is something older than memory—dwells in us—
that remembers its history in ancient blood—
a tale—
that has no words—
only the immediacy of this meeting—
the woman—and this other—this wolf—

this bright white Arctic face—
this thick and brindled coat of fur—

that tenuous thread—linking—one to the other—
and the uncountable centuries of Alone.

# HAIKU
*for Jude and Thello*

Sacred unions
remember the labyrinth
in all its turnings—

# FOREST RITUAL
*for Jan Buchner and Kin*

The after-rain forest is fresh with the scent of pine and damp earth.

It is early morning—a little after eight.
I have the dogs with me—a blue-eyed Husky—
and a sleek black Rescue Special—
one a free spirit—
the other my devoted shadow.
We are here for a short spell of sunshine.
The forecast for the remainder of the day is rain.

We have just come to an opening in the forest
—a place of startling light
—a cutting
—a wide swathe of open ground—between two dark stands of trees.

What sets it apart from other such pathways—
is the coarse, white texture of the sand.
Today—still wet—it glistens
with brightness.

The panting—pink-tongue dogs
—ahead of me—
are sniffing out the morning scent-messages.

I am about to cross this shining whiteness—
when—at my feet—I see a large paw-print—
close to the cutting's edge—
just beyond the shadow of the tall dark trees.

The print—made after the rain had stopped
—is fresh
—and clean.

I know the young man who owns the pure-bred wolf
—terrified of dogs—he told me.
He comes to the forest
—early—
before the dogs arrive.

I am almost certain that the large print
has been left by this wolf.

I walk away from the cutting—
call the dogs—
and make my way back to the car.

Back at home I find a bowl—and a large kitchen ladle.

I return to the forest—to the cutting—to the paw-print.

I love ritual.
The heightened sense—of presence—of reverence.
The awareness of the respect that is required
for each and every act of grace.

This may not be rushed.

I place the bowl and ladle—close to the print.
I kneel down.
The cold wetness presses through my jeans.

I ask the forest for permission to take the paw-print and the coarse soil that
supports it—
that I consider this to be a sacred mission—
that I will always hold this forest fragment with respect.

I wait—

I listen to the forest sounds—
for a sign
—offered perhaps—
by some wolf or forest deity.

Nothing.
There is a strange hush.

And then—the startling—harsh cry of a hadeda overhead.

I bow my head.
I bend forward over the paw-print.
I take care not to disturb even one grain of sand with my knees.
I lift the print and put it into the bowl.
Now—I take the area of sand
that shows the swift after-trace of the foot—as he raced across the
cutting—
and add it to the rest.

There are no other paw-prints.
The cutting is a place—favoured by many riders—
the sand is churned up—and soft.
It will not show
—with any clarity—
the trajectory of his path.

This happened—twenty-five years ago.

Today—
as I write this—
I have on my desk a hand-made earthenware bowl.

In it—
the bright, white, decomposed granite from the cutting
—still flashes its crystal-like facets of forest light—

a flash of sacred—
and soul—
and wild—

# THE LAST WOLF—THE LAST WORD
*for Alaska*

She was the last wolf
brindled coat—a haunting white face
her name was Alaska
we met thirteen years ago
now she is gone

he brought flowers the day after she died
two full-blown irises in the bunch
I will remember them—
and him—

but that is only one way of telling the story.

We first met in 1942 in Canada during World War II
I was alone in a dark room, and she came to me
we have walked together for seventy-seven years.

Now we walk on beneath the northern wheel of heaven
vast white wastes
pristine snow
and forests

walking wild

following that One True Star

## ONE STEP AWAY FROM WILD

How I love your shape-shift dance
So full of child
And the narrow line you walk
One step away from wild

Your ancestry lingers
Behind your eyes
Silent as snowfall
Silent as moonrise

You turn your white face to me
And I am undone
With your lonely howl
My heart is lost—and won

A cold wind blowing over snow
Uncorrupted and undefiled
Has put a spirit into you
One step away from wild

# ALASKA

A thousand years of silence sleep
in those dark eyes—
and centuries of Arctic dreams.

In what white forest did you first open your eyes
and know it to be your country?

Out of what sleek night
—silent with moon and shadows—
were you born?

What clean wind
first filled your ears and nostrils
with its scent of ice and wild?

And—
what untouchable inheritance
remembers you—
in the haunting echoes of your howl?

# RAVEN

What is this dark bird
if not an emissary—
an augur from the underworld
or from the crypt of night—
who tells a rosary
—slow bede by slow bede—
—and many turnings—
in the labyrinthine tapestry
of my heart?

# HAIKU

As the world lay hushed
in day's first kiss—a dark bird
flew across the sun.

## No Stars! No Moon!

No stars—no moon—this raven night
dreams me pinioned
in shamanic flight

## Sap Rising in an Old Tree

Sap rising in an old tree—
what does it serve?
Only the blossom knows—

## STRANGE MEETING

Behind the shadows—
a wounding
and the wildness breaking
in him
like a storm—

with stretched-out soul—
and feral concentration—
in his eye—

he came
—this unbroken one—

and I to meet him—
in that strange
fierce land—


## HAIKU

He is no stranger—
this dark keeper of my fate—
my one certainty—

# INITIATION

A mark of passage—this small tattoo—
this wolf footprint and scarlet winged heart
—indelibly blazoned over sacred bone—
sanctifies my entry into the new country.

I know now
—as I have not known before—
that the world will not own me—

that this small, chosen stain
—bestowed on me by grace—
stands over and against
—all thou shalt nots
—all compliance
—all that would
corrupt
silence
or
enslave.

For the watchful spirit that entered me
—when I was but a child—
the fur—the flesh—and bone of him—
the keen eyes looking out through mine
his urgent breath
the guard-hairs
prickling down my spine—

remembers an older law—
a clean attention.

An inherent instinct
that refuses to be betrayed.

# BELIEF
*Mid-winter on the Tres Piedras Pass. New Mexico*

In this high thin place of pristine whiteness
—of snow-drifts—
—lonely reaches—
—emptiness—
and cold

with all around a blood-stained heaven—on fire and dying—
I am confronted by a solitude
whose utter stillness—
terrifies.

Here—
all sound is silenced but the raw breath of the wind
—a bone-cold keening that haunts the hollow places—
and the faint blue traces
—that betray the silent crossings—
are the marks of those who honour
an indifferent god.

This is the ancient world of immediacy.

Here—
instinct
is a passion
swifter than thought.

A world of one law
—a single clean attention—
a law that will not sanction
the indulgence of belief.

# SNOW
*for Leigh and Ian Koenigsfest.*
*Vancouver, December 2005*

In the gorge
a cutting stream of glass-clear water
flows swift and cold
to fall on clean rock—
its thunder
muffled to a whisper.

Hemlock and cedar
stand
—still as gods—
—and reach up through drifts of mist and spray—
to touch a low white sky
narrow
and thin
with cold.

Nothing moves.
No other eye meets mine.

I stand—
small—bone-cold—and infinitely vulnerable—
the animal compulsions of my blood
—overwhelmed—
by the empty stare of this frozen mask.

    Yet—
 I must bow in deep respect—
  bow to this cold presence
   even as I fear it—
  bow to this shining face
 with its terrible immediacy.

But it is the utter silence of the snow that so appals me—

   appals me with its beauty—

  the awful beauty of this silence—
 this terrifying muting of the world—
  this soft white sleep that can kill.


## HAIKU

There is no silence
I know—more absolute than
the silence of snow—

# THE CUTTING EDGE

Snow has fallen.

All night the raven sits in his frozen tree—
a dark hunch—
silent as black.

All night he listens to the snarls of pain—
the yelps and cries—
the small and awful gnawing.

Morning and a pale sky—
the winter forest glistens with hard light—
trees etch themselves
—black and bare—
against the stare of snow.

In the clearing
—cold light on cold steel—
an empty pool of snow—turned scarlet.

Footprints in the snow
three footprints
—and a thin scarlet line.
And silence.

Silent as shadow—
silent as black—
the raven lights upon cold steel—
reaches his black beak over the pool of scarlet—
over the scarlet snow—

and with practice—
and precision—
he extricates the blood-offering
from the steel jaw.

## BIRTHRIGHT

Within us there are stories etched in bone—
and memories.
In the dark cave of the skull
each totem animal
—image of blood—
treads out the patterns
old as stars.

In their mothers' bellies
the slow fish remember their scales
—and swim that urgent stream—
shedding gills and tails
—that fall away—
that long black falling
into the blackness of night.

There is a rage that hides in that dark place
where the black water
rises and falls
rises and falls

where a soul
—pale and naked—
stands shouting at the night
in that place of darkness and forgotten tears.

If only we will offer ourselves to the mercy of that night.
If only our senses lead us down into that dark earth—
we will find in the imprints
—and in the memories of our beginnings—
the compassion of a world
old as stars.

# SUZIE-NOSIZWE – MPHEPHO
### for Suzie Nosizwe

The travel-stained Land Rover pulls up outside the house.
A woman jumps out, and strides over to where I am standing at the gate.
My first impression is one of incredible energy.

"Hello, Gorgeous Being," she says.

She is dressed in a traditional skirt and is wearing her Sangoma beads.
A kikoi[2] is slung over one shoulder.
She carries an ichoba[3].

Before I can respond, she looks at me closely.
"You need *mphepho*,[4]" she says. "I have some in the car."

She returns with an armful of the shrub.
It has grey leaves, and small, yellow flowers.

"You burn this in the house. Breathe it in deeply. Also, boil it and add to the water of your bath.
Occasionally, make a cup of tea from it—only one.
It is good for pain and headaches."
She hands me the bundle.

"Hello, Suzie," I say, as I take the large bunch. "Come in and—"

---

2  *Kikoi*: a colourful African cloth
3  *Ichoba*: fly whisk
4  *Mphepho*: one of Africa's sacred herbs.

"Can't stay," she says. "I have dogs in the car."

And she is gone.

# HAIKU

Two shining mirrors—
each reflecting back the light!
And—the source of it?



# HAIKU
*for Suzie Nosiswe*

I dreamed you brought me
—a pitch-black Eagle Feather—
"Fly on," you said. "Fly—"



# HAIKU
*for Ann Lamprecht*

In her quietness
—Queen of Synchronicity—
makes good things happen.

# THE ALOE RITUALS

It has become a point of power for us—this place close to the tall aloes in our garden. It has been identified as the place of healing power by a sangoma known to us, and it is now the place where we burn *mphepho* to mark some passage in our lives, or in the life of a friend.

It is marked by a large earthenware bowl with deep, vertical sides. This, in turn, stands on an upturned garden pot, bringing the bowl to altar height. In its simplicity it easily blends into its surroundings.

The first two rituals were for Glenda and Thompson. They attended a course during which the group was invited to experience a closed-eye journey, up a mountain path and into a cave. There, they would meet a wise old man and ask a question.

But Thompson's "wise old man" was not in a cave. Nor was he up the mountain. He was sitting next to a river. Thompson asked him if he could drink from the river, but the old man shook his head. He reached down and produced an ancient wooden goblet.

"Do you see that river over there?" he said, pointing to where a second river was flowing swiftly, some distance away. "You must only drink from that river."

He handed the goblet over to Thompson, who then continued on his journey.

Thompson thought that maybe he had got it wrong. We heard something else—that this was a time to slow down, to explore the depth of the message in this strange meeting.

\*

A phone call was made to a woodcarver in Knysna, requesting a wooden goblet be carved bearing the ancient designs of such goblets.

The goblet duly arrived.

We gathered under the tall aloe and waited for Thompson to join us.

We reminded him of his experience, and then the *mphepho* was lit.

The fragrant smoke drifted over us.

Thompson was given the goblet to mark the ritual, while Jacques sang for him.

The goblet now held the question of the other river.

When Glenda was still living in Zimbabwe there was a young girl, Nyasha, who was very ill, and deteriorating under the family's care. It was with relief that they gave her to Glenda to nurse. They did not expect Nyasha to get better.

But with regular visits to the clinic, good food and the love she was receiving, Nyasha soon began to improve. Because the clinic was quite a distance away, and Glenda had to carry Nyasha on her back, it was hard work. But the nursing, together with the necessary medication, soon showed results.

When the family noticed this, they said they wanted the young girl to return to them. They didn't approve of the clinic, and they would take her back to the traditional healer.

Nyasha was duly taken back. But not before she thanked Glenda, with tears in her eyes, and said she wanted to give her a goat. This would have been the customary gift to express gratitude. But Nyasha had no money to buy a goat, and it would appear that the family did not consider it important, although culturally it could have been expected.

It was a sad parting for Glenda when the family came to take Nyasha home again. Not long afterwards Nyasha died.

In her telling of the story, Glenda shed tears. But not for herself. The tears were for Nyasha, who died without being able to do this one thing—to give Glenda a white goat.

It so happened that we had a white, beaded goat in the garden—beaded by men from Zimbabwe, working not far from the house.

And so, the *mphepho* was lit, and the gift of a white goat was given in Nyasha's name—and the smoke drifted up, bringing the blessing of closure with it.

## BONES AND SHADOWS

Except you know what bones can tell
—and the dark earth—
you will be a stranger to yourself.

Bones—
even as they bleach and rattle in the wind
even though they lie buried under dirt and stone
bones carry the knowing.

If you would speak with bones
you must let the darkness take you down—
beyond that place where the thin light
—cold as dawn on scree—
struggles to hold—
beyond even the memory of light.

If you would speak with bones—if you have the heart for it—
all must be surrendered.

Only emptiness will carry you beyond that primal moment—
when a rough beast
—first split the world—
—beyond the cave—
into a place so old it has forgotten itself.

If you would know that clean rage
—that burns in the eye of each wild creature—
—if you would take that forbidden step—

—cross that line—
—and enter the ancient world of immediacy—
you must surrender that keen blade that separates the worlds.

Do not be fooled by shadows—
despair is not the deepest place you may go.

# DANCE
*for John Faul*

I don't know which was the more wild
—an even pair—
so matched were they.

He—
a mix of Celtic blood—and dark—and poetry
—an animal of Ireland.

She—
of the far north
—so very nearly wolf—
but come to meet in a foreign place
through creaturely recognition.

It was a dance they did that day—
the day she gave her heart to him—
gave her will to that tall man
—that gangly Nureyev—
—gave over her will—
fixed that white and wolf-like mask
—the ice-blue eyes—
on his—
and never faltered.

I have the print of it behind my eyes
—indelible—
can see the dance as though it were yesterday.

And she not dead.
And he not crippled with pain.
And the years between not flown.

# HER LAST PASSAGE
*for Mischka, 2005*

This business of dying requires patience.
It will not be hurried.

I watch the gradual loss of that once energetic instinct
and the slow ebb of vitality and impulse
—like these thin winter days—
growing shorter now—
and cold—
and the memory of summer
a faint tracery of veins
—etched—
in the skeletons of leaves.

Her once sturdy form is now defined by angles—
the bone-structure—
palpable beneath the Arctic fur.

The supple lope has left her—
so too the careless confidence.
And her step has lost its sureness
and its symmetry.

There is an extraordinary dignity about her now
—a new presence—
even in the wasted form.
And poignant moments of confusion
—or apology—
that her proud spirit should require assistance.

I watch
—while she sleeps—
the soft rise and fall of her breathing
—each out-breath taking with it—
an hour—a day—a lifetime—

and the slow tide of last things
—gathering in—
the unravelling devotions of her soul.

# THE ANCESTORS
*for Mischka, 2005*

It is the time of gathering.
Once again I am walking with the dead.

They are all around me now
—and drawing in—
this shape-shift throng of powerful otherness—
this energetic presence
—neither human nor creature—
dark angels of ancient descent.

They have assembled here to gather in their own—
this single
—not-quite-wolf creature that I love—
this fierce spirit of uncompromised affections.

No amount of love can hold her now.

And—
even though I now have some knowing of their ways—
even though death is in some manner known to me—
even though I no longer fear their visitations—
even so—
this grief divides me.

Her world has grown small—
too small for such wildness.

The few stumbling steps from the stairwell where she sleeps
to the high-walled seclusion of the yard
—and on sunny afternoons—to her kilim on the paving—
overlooking the waters of the vlei[5].

It is a long—slow—waiting
—and not done yet—
a painful time—intimate—and beautiful.

My world has fallen into hers.
I stay close to her now—
listening to the light—
breathing in the transience of each timeless day—
and the bitter-sweet passions of memory.

---

5  *Vlei:* a small shallow lake

# STRANGE

The night is pregnant with the dead.
The veil between the worlds is thin.

There is a gathering in the shadows of this house—
this new and unfamiliar place to which I have come—
this house—this town—this empty night—
and the night-streets that echo the town's indifference.

I am a stranger here.

Only the watchful dead are familiar now
and they press in on me—with their urgent voices
—and the weight of memory—
these voices that I love.

And these faces—
a flood of presences—crowding me with tears
—tearing the veil—
so that I struggle in my mind to hold the worlds apart.

I could step across this narrow divide.
It is no distance at all
—the merest blink—
this forbidden crossing—
and find—
what?

The almost touch—
the Husky coat—

the pricked ears—
the ice and shadow of those pale blue northern eyes.

Breathe again that wildness
with its taste of blood.

It is not for people that I grieve.
That work is done.

It is for this other country—
this undivided place of soul—
so strange
so wild.

Everything in me grieves
for this other kinship—

this other kin of mine—

# MEMORY

I feel her slip away from me
to drift
insubstantial as mist
back to her white world origins.

Now
grief and memory
have become numbed
—and muted—
—the way snow covers the wounds of a landscape—
until the true shape of things vanishes
—and memory has become a fabrication of desire—
a death that will not die
—a haunting—
—a wound—
I yet carry in my heart
—that will not leave me—

# THE COLOUR OF SHADOWS

Already I know—as you do not
—who dwell in that bright eternal present—
that a day will come when I shall walk alone
among these tall pines
—and look for you—

will search
—beyond the cutting—
between the so-familiar pathways
—that you have made your own—
for that white face turned towards me
—that fleeting form—
vanishing into the silence of forest—

will search—
will find—
only the absence of you—

a memory—
the colour of shadows—

## HAIKU

What are these shadows
that lie behind my seeing?
Footprints of the night.

## HAIKU

Would you know the truth?
Go listen to the dark wind—
it will not tell you.

## THE PRESENCE OF ABSENCE

### I Look for Her in the Forest

I look for her in the forest—
the dog who died—
she is everywhere—

### How Full the Bright Moon

How full the bright moon—
how still the dark night—
how silent the howling dog—

# LOBO

It is the absence of him that haunts me—
so that I listen
only
for that single drawn-out note that calls—
has always called—
that echoes in my brain like a madness.

So that I long for that uncorrupted solitude
—to feel that fierce wild eye upon me—
feel it pierce me
through and through
a wound to cleave me
from the too-much world.

I long to feel the sensuous touch of that electric fur
—the vibrant nerve of his immediacy—
breathe in that sweet breath
that sings me back to nakedness.

I want to take the path of mountain wind—
I want to dare that hawk-wing sky of emptiness—
to fly alone.

Better to die alone in a high place
than ignore such a calling.

Some matings are for life.

# WOLF MOUNTAIN

No one visits Wolf Mountain.
No one is invited.

He lives surrounded by the architecture of isolation—
high—thin—places
—edges of forests—
the company of shadows.

He knows well the silence of mountains—
the emptiness of mountain wind.

His eyes reflect
—the cold clean circle of night—
—the detachment of moon—
the indifferent stars.

It is this self-same solitude
—has shaped his song—
has written into his heart the sound of alone.

He has learnt not to need the company of strangers—
not to need mirrors—
not to need consolation.

He has become
—over many years—
a fierce disciple in the art of singleness.

But should fate intervene—

should another enter his world—
should the stranger arrive
—by an unseen path—
and steal beneath the guard of his uncorrupted wildness—

should some agency—
some need
—perhaps we might call it love—
ever mirror back to him the face of his aloneness—

how then would all this solitary beauty endure?

# HOWL

So how can it be
that I
a wolf
—skilled in solitude and high thin places—
should now so tremble for the sweetness of your embrace?

That the memory of you
—your voice—
—your song—
should so resonate within me—
a resonance that haunts me to the bone?

That this shudder of wind
—that strips my heart of all its shadows—
—that strips me bare of all that splendid isolation—
is come
—at last—
fierce and ruthless?

So that I stand naked as desire.
So that all winds may find me.

Yet—
I long only to surrender that solitude
—to leave those isolated wastes—
and—terrified with beauty
—and the wonder of it—
offer to you
—the most precious thing I own—

the raw
unguarded
and uncorrupted howl
of my love.

## THE HERESY

        Tonight—
    the veil is thin that separates the worlds—
and the country of the dead seems close to me.

        Tonight—
       I almost see her face
    —the white mask—that piercing stare—
        and feel
      just beneath my skin
    —the pricked and prickling stand of hair—
and her wild and Arctic silence steal through me.

        Tonight—
   there is a presence in the shadows—
    and I hear—or almost hear
      —my father's voice—
      —so close it seems—

—I could reach out and touch its resonance—

        Tonight—
    the veil is thin that separates the worlds—

and I feel the strong tug of death's persuasion—
this compelling summons to what is hidden—
    this always fascination that I have
      with what is other—and forbidden.

So strong
—the invitation to step through the shroud of this divide—

and now that grief has rolled away the stone
and rent the veil that isolates the dead—

I hear that terrible—and not to be denied command—

and that awful keening sound
—that keens and keens and keens—
and never ends—
until
I take this step

and
—heretic to the last—

enter the forbidden land.

## HAIKU

Call him the dark guest—
I have come to know his touch—
it is a comfort—

## HAIKU

Drawing closer now—
so close—like a lover—this
other kin of mine—

# LIVING MY DYING

I am living my dying
—blown through by desert wind—
torn apart
—by the ever-expanding circle of a vast horizon—
and the complicated longings
of blood and bone.

I am living my dying
—crucified on thorns of fierce desire—
a tree lit with holiness
and dread
and always the beauty in it.

A strange alchemy—
waiting to find completion.

It is not enough that we die—
death alone is no final note
no last word to end all complaint—

But to live it
—never to bend the knee—
to live our dying
—like the slow ageing of a fine red wine—
to arrive—at last
—a magnificent libation—

Till death itself bows down
before such grace.

# TESTAMENT

How may we ever dare to love
—small beings that we are—
finite
and full of limitation?

For surely we must hear the laughter
of the gods
and shudder
beneath infinity's vast gaze
—bow our heads—
—and kneel in awe—
dazzled by the omnipotence
of these inscrutable divinities.

And yet—
I take this step
out of the cast of solitude—
throw out the last that has shod
and bound me to a crippled path—

I take this step—
this defiant stride of faith
into the testament of love.

# LEAVING THE WORLD

I wanted to show you the world
of mist and mountain

—wanted you to feel that silence—

to take you far from streets and houses
and small rooms
from the smallness of all that was familiar.

And so we left behind all conversation
and sat together
—beyond the fevered world—
while the mist rolled down its veils of silence
into a place made mute
by whiteness.

We uttered no word.

And I watched
the slow wonder light your face
and the wetness
breathe a film of stars into your hair.

And you were all there was that day
—of blood and bone—

and the white mist around you.

## HAIKU

Thick mist mutes the world—
and still the small voice whispers
in the white silence

## A RARE BLUE FLOWER

I have spent my life
walking the edges of precipices
searching always
for a rare blue flower
that may
or may not
exist.

Sometimes I fall.

I can show you the scars.

I am so tired of precipices.
I am so tired of falling.

When may I come down from these high thin places
and find a field of untidy crimson poppies
blowing careless as laughter
in the wind?

# THE RIVER BENEATH THE RIVER

Let us enter once more
the river of old wounds

and be amazed to find
—beneath its shining surface—
the wide-eyed
silent fish

drawn by urgent memory
—and the fierceness of instinct—

swimming—upstream
—steady and silver—
between
the dark stepping-stones of faith.

# THE ART OF AUGURY

How may we read the woven stories of our lives—
or count with flint upon a stone—
the true number of our years?

Or recognise that narrow path
—that weaves like golden thread—
a river
through the landscape of our days—

forsake our fears and indecision
—entreat the nightly skies—
certain that the star that draws us on
is faithful
in ways we cannot comprehend?

Surely we have not lost the art of augury—
and may yet read our fate
among those stars
—or listen to the wind blow through our dreams—
and know the patterned language of a bird's swift flight—

might know from these
—the shape-shift nature of our lives—
and throw ourselves
like easy dice
—certain of that return—
and so make light of all adversity
the gods may send.

I do remember
as a child
—I knew such things—

could hear the wild-speak tongue of creatures
water—
wind—
lived in a world that breathed into my heart.

And now it seems
that I have lost the art—
and hear only the world's intrusive currency.

Yet—
I do still have those secret corners in my life
—beyond such fluency—
where bones are hid in shadows
and places where I bury treasures
that the world may not make shame
with scorn
their innocent simplicity.

I listen to the silent speech of stones
when I am alone
—I do not apologise for my duplicity.

But I grieve for that lost and sacred art—
that place of knowing innocence
within the heart.

# RITE

I need my wildness now—

to find
—that holy intuition—

unburdened by the weight
of self-imposed
shackles—
or what the world may think—

to step
into the authorship
—of this one shining life—
which is the right of every living thing—

and to relinquish
all desire for mercy.

## HAIKU

In deepest silence
—and not in the spoken word—
the secret whispers.


## HAIKU

I can hear the call—
how it thunders in my heart—
yet it has no word—

## WHAT IS THE CALL?

I cannot see your face
The dark holds me in its prayer
And I hear you calling
And you are everywhere

This calling of the heart
It breaks every rule
I come blinded by love
Naked as a fool

And the night is huge and silent
Inside my brain
And I hear you calling me
I hear you speak my name

What is the word my lips cannot utter?
What is this dark prayer holds me in its thrall?
What is the name my heart can only stutter?
What is the call?

# THE GEOMETRY OF FATE

He marks the geometry of his fate
in blood upon the sand—
and suffers the punishment of the pics
that swing above the wound—
and seeks out
his *querencia*[6]
in the heat-thick afternoon.

He marks the geometry of his fate
on the yellow Mexican sand.
A purple shadow casts a pall—
and blood scarlets the wound—
and still
the slow figure with the cape
like a lover
draws him round.

A fierce ancestry has bred into him
—this bloodshot and fated hour—
bred into him
—this splendid rage—
this geometric law—
this bloodshot focus on the man—
the still matador.

His head swings low
—that great muscle weakened by the wound—
his heaving flanks

---

6  *Querencia*: Bull's place of preference in the ring.

—spattered with blood—
　　his great strength unwound.

　　The bloodshot eye is slow—
the great horns—close to the ground.

　　　　The air is so still.

　　The crowd is silent on its feet.
　　Two arcs of fate have met.
　　The geometry is complete.
　　　A rush of dark wind
　　　　　—a hush—
　　　　a blood-instinct
　　　—so swift—so sweet—

　one sideways thrust of the horn
finds the matador—dead on his feet.

# SACRAMENT

A dark wind is eating me
I feel it in my bones
This fierce communion
This shuddering black song

Oh what rapture! What rapture!
This night without a moon
This fierce communion
This shuddering black song

What is this hunger that holds me in its thrall?
This love that so corrupts me?
This song with the black night in it
That so undoes me?

A dark wind is eating me
I feel it in my bones
This fierce communion
This shuddering black song

## AN INVISIBLE PATH

Day breaks
—always at the edge of itself—
and draws a thin pale line against the darkness

and we who lie dreaming
—are nudged over that liminal edge—
while the dream falls like a stone
—unseen—
into the well of night.

This dawn moment
—this half-sleep—
—this almost union—
comes so close to it.

But it is not union
—this soft pattern of meeting—with the parting already in it—
—this soft illusion—
so fiercely intangible
that only a bird may fly through it.

And so—
I hold to solitude
—and walk alone the shadowy animal of night—
drawn like a lover
—to its dark illuminations—
its penumbral mystery.

# AUGURY

How shall I know myself?

Shall I read my soul in the flight patterns of wild geese?
Shall I turn to the dark earth
and find
—older than bones and shadows—
the slow
and hidden
groping of my origins?

Shall I invite the wind
—seduce the stars from out their orbits—
beseech the ocean's inscrutable waters
to give me answer?

Every angel would caution me—
every angel knows the price of too much passion.

Yet—
part of what I am
is this urgent question.

How can I not challenge the gods
even as I bow to them?

# BLACK FIRE

I know what it is to dance at the edge of madness
—to challenge the gods' omnipotence—
and suffer their fierce rage
for such irreverent heresy.

I have tasted that black fire
—that eats away our human certainty—
and know what it is to fall
from life's intoxicating heights—

to slough false skin
—into that place of bones and shadow—
until the soul is
shriven
of all its passions.

And yet—
I dance and dance again
—drawn by that madness that will accept no other law—
than to be itself—

the madness that does not supplicate
—when death grins and beckons—
but answers to the darkest bidding of the heart—

and will descend
—if summoned—
into hell itself
and dance

this heretical
fierce
art.

# GOD'S EYE VIEW

I stand now
—close to the ruin of my days—
while dark birds
with their too-wide-open eyes
fall from the sky
in urgent and un-patterned flight.

What is this too-fast heartbeat
of the world—
what animal is it
—beautiful and terrible—
now wrests itself once more from sleep?

And these dark emissaries
—with un-shuttered eyes—
what do they see from that place
of high blue flight—

how the web of things
trembles
on the brink of night?


# A High Place—Blue Sky

A high place—blue sky
—and silence everywhere—
the day the sun went out

# LIZARD BRAIN

There is a cold black stare—
an eye that does not close—
a thin slit of a grin
that holds no humour.

The old lizard watches
—from his cold keep—
just beneath the cave of reason.

Where are we now
with all our letters—
and our conquests—
and our fail-safe strategies?

What will it take for us to own
this hidden face?

To grasp—

that there is nothing
more dangerous than an exiled rage—

nothing more powerful
than the unknown?

## An Ancient Lizard Slumbers

An ancient lizard slumbers—
curled like a root—
at the base of my skull

# FIERCE
### for Ian McCallum

Who is this upstart infant so lately found in Eden?
This new arrival—this naked one
—who must perforce cover his nakedness with clothing?

Who is said to worship a god?

A brilliant creature—
one might say inventive—
visionary—

Well so he is!

And look at that bright new tool he brings
—that mirror of the mind that gazes inward—
so reflectively!

This hairless one
—who beats his proud chest—
this pinnacle of creation
—this almost-god—
beyond all innate tricks and ploys of nature's patterning

—or so he would believe.

And look at that thumb
—or does he fool himself—
this shape-shift creature—
this very recent guest?

Certainly he walks upright
—on two legs—
and keeps his claws well-hidden—
and his tail.

And when he shows his teeth
—it is to smile—
and is known to laugh
—sometimes at himself—

and yet—?

and yet—?

He is well-versed in all of nature's skilful games—
how well he knows them—
and practices deception with the rest.

And—
look a little behind that tempered manner
—that intellect that plans—
—and waits—
that can delay
for years
—if necessary—
its kill.

And look again into those eyes

—look a little deeper

—there's the blood

—and there's the old lizard who never sleeps.

Do not be fooled.
Beneath a sometimes very thin veneer—
everything is fierce.

# THE FIERCE WILD ANARCHY OF DREAMS
*for Joan Brokensha*

How do we dare presume to know this strange language
that comes to us in dreams—
these images
—the early dawn blood and bone of them—
that haunt the shadowy caverns of our skulls?

These ancient creatures—drawn in blood—
knew their landscape
savage—wild—and innocent
long before we stood upright—
long before the slowness of thinking—
long before
the slowness of speech could stutter out the first groping words
of human thought.

Out of what ancient dawn—
from what mist of un-measured beginning
where no rules were written—
where survival was an elemental law
and territory held its claim—

out of what kind of instinct for balance
did they hold their pattern
for hundreds of thousands of years?

And now the laws are written in stone.
And where the fierce innocence now?

# PORTRAIT
*for Sharon McCallum*


It is the angle of the head that arrests us
—the slight turning—
so subtle you might miss it.
And something about the inclination of the neck—
at once familiar
and yet
—strange—
and the barest suggestion of a self-imposed steadiness
—a quality of alert anticipation—
which evokes our curiosity.

The seated figure looks small—
dwarfed by what stands behind.
The chair
—incongruous in this setting—
so too the tea-mug
resting on the wooden arm.

The hands that hold the work
—are raised—
—slightly towards the face—
the fingers caught
—motionless—
in their deft slip-and-flick action down the knitted row.

The backdrop—
—a tall tangle of wilderness—
is puzzling

—as is the shadowy presence—
which incredulity instantly deletes.

There is a marvellous serenity about the scene—
a peace that comes when one so fills a space with beingness—
that no harm can intrude.

A moment of utter stillness—
simple
and profound.

But—
who is it rakes this cloud of dust
—this red-earth aura that fills the clearing—
with
—yes—
holy light?

Who is it demonstrates his territorial claim—
and then
—magnanimously—
permits
the impudent intrusion?

Witness if you will
—this authentic participation—
woman and elephant
in
poetic conversation.

# LINYANTI
*for Ian McCallum*

It is an unusual consulting-room.
So too the location.

To qualify—
you must be conversant with instinct—
and be prepared to follow an ancient trail—
tracks set in red earth
dust
and memory.

It might be best to have four legs
—but two will suffice—
or a hairy coat—or stripes—or splotches
perhaps a trunk
—at the very least—
a beak and feathers
or a slithering silence
and scales.

Certainly, you must have retained your wildness.
Without it—
you will not remember this landscape.

And respect
—this would be an essential quality—
as would a vigilant attention.

The hours are not confined to daytime—

and many a wondrous encounter
takes place beneath a fat African moon
—and a night sky—
breathless and silent—sown and seeded with stars.

And there is of course
—that last-light threshold hour—
when the hushed land lingers in silhouette
—against a sky of blood and fire—
—breathing its beauty—
so loud
you can hear the silence.

Grunts—cackles—calls—roars
—hoots and howls—
and the like
are most certainly encouraged.

But—
in all instances of curiosity—
stillness must be maintained.

At all times—
you must consider who will be the teacher.

It is called the talking cure by some
—here it is all about listening—
with every pricked sense
in spirited communion.

Most especially
the heart.

# BARS

I am a poet in a cage.

Does it matter how I came here?
Does it matter who made the bars?
Wild things do not survive such ruthless penning.
Imagination soon dies in such a place.

I am a poet in a cage
—so full of bars—
I cannot hear the beating of my heart.
Have lost the wind that breathes me.

Have forgotten
how the world once turned
—so full of fire—
and
—fragments of beauty—
that I wept for its loveliness.

Now my eyes are full of bars
—of steel impediments—
that close upon my heart
—that never bend—

and like that panther—
I am grown so weary
—even of desire—

yet pace to the exhausted edges
of myself
—each day—
haunted
by emptiness.

# FIRE

All those heretics
—who have dared to touch the fire—
and claim it for their own—

who have stalked the fierceness of night—
have haunted the utterance of wind—

they will know—

All those—
who have descended deep into the dark earth
—beyond all light—
beyond even the memory
of light—

they too will know—

All who have taken
—if only one step—
across that forbidden threshold—

will know—

they will know
the rage
that smoulders—

just beneath the surface of their human face.

# YOU'VE GOT TO STEP OUT THE BOAT

You've got to step out the boat
You want to walk on water
Got to get your feet wet
Just to taste the fire
And the holy bush—it will brand you
When you touch its flame
And you'll never go back
To that old world again

They say I'm a sinner
I've gone broken my slate—
Get down on your knees—they say
Before it's too late
But I've shed my shoes
And a blue fire calls—
My feet are on the water
And the old world—it falls

They talk about a madman
He's gone lost his way
No one can save him now
That's what they say
But I'm barefoot on the water
I hear the angels call
I'm dancing in the fire
And the old world—it falls

You've got to step out the boat
You want to walk on water

Got to get your feet wet
Just to taste the fire
And the holy bush—it will brand you
When you touch its flame
And you'll never go back
To that old world again

# THE DARK WIND

Poets live for it.
Heretics have died for it.
Every bullfighter knows it.
Everyone who lives close to the edge.

Anyone—
who loves beauty more than life itself—
anyone—
who has dared to challenge death—
will know
—this dark wind that whispers in the heart—
that blows through us
its terrifying beauty.

In the end it is all about beauty—
and our whispered conversations with death.

## HAIKU

All around me now—
a gathering of my kin—
drawing in the night—


## HAIKU

How long is a life?
Always the dark wind whispers
beneath the threshold—


## HAIKU

You never leave me
—invisible though you be—
pain—my lonely kin.

# ANCESTRY

We—
who are human
—products of civilisation—
some kind of elevated species
—supposedly higher than the rest—
we—
who have lost our senses
—and most of our sense—
pride ourselves on our achievements—

so that—now
we barely shudder
—when a shadow passes over us—
the hair that used to prickle
down the whole long length of us
—now—
barely stands.

Now—
vaguely—
we feel disquieted at the sight of blood—
and absent-mindedly smooth our hair—
unaware as we do this of the fierce centuries
of our ancestry.

What have we done with our authentic rage—

>           that
>           clean
>           clear
>           light?
>
>         So fierce—
>        so ruthless—

# THE MERCY OF WILD THINGS

A wild breath is breathing me
An old pulse at the base of my skull
A longing in the cave of my mind
And it's tugging at my soul

I have to leave this house of moths and butterflies
With all its births and unwritten endings
Find my way back into the fierce world
And the mercy of wild things

Find my way back to a place that's older than memory
That ancient solitude that sings
And the great herds thundering in my blood
And the mercy of wild things

# THE ICONOCLAST

We shed our skins
—again and again—
until we die.

We shed our skins
until we lie
—naked of all deceit—
mirrored in the still waters of reflection

—and find—
laid bare beneath our many unguents
—and soothing oils—
the ancient wound
unhealed.

When did the footprints of the black wind
first break the surface of that teeming pond
and
—shatter—
into a thousand splintering shards
the image of our face?

What fascination is it—
what instinct—
draws us down?

And what is it—
slides and slithers
—cold and scaly—
just beneath the gilded icon of our conceit?

What is it grins up at us
—that thin reptilian cut of smile—
that cold unshuttered stare?
What is this scaly creature
with a tail
—this cold and fierce inheritance—
that waits—
and waits—
beneath the thin veneer of thought?

What is this unreflecting impulse
—that throats in blood—
its guttural rage at death?

# A BLUE PIG FROM MEXICO

I bought a wooden pig in a marketplace in Mexico
I bought a wooden pig and he's painted sky and blue
I carry him on my shoulder though his weight is heavy
I carry him though he's heavy back home to you

I carry on my shoulders the sky of Mexico
I carry on my lips a song of blue
But my heart—ah love—my heart I leave in Mexico
I bring only the sky of Mexico to you

I carry a wooden pig and his face is fat and happy
He's strong in his heart and his love is fierce and true
His belly is fat and round like the bright sun of Mexico
I carry him though he's heavy back home to you

I carry on my shoulders the sky of Mexico
I carry on my lips a song of blue
But my heart—ah love—my heart I leave in Mexico
I bring only the sky of Mexico to you

## RANCHO DE SAN JUAN—NEW MEXICO

First light.

The desert lies as if beneath a veil. Untouched.

Only the furthest ridges are visible, more an obscure vagary of the light than an actual form.

The air is cold.

My nostrils fill with the scent of juniper and piñon, and dew-damp earth.

Because of the mesa's height and my close proximity to it, I will not see the sunrise; only its effects.
I watch the infinitesimal shifting of the light, almost imperceptible, as it slants over the land: a slow and sensitive exploration, like a lover discovering his beloved's breast for the first time.

As the sun gains elevation and the light grows stronger, the first tinges of warmth and colour appear. Slowly the multiple layers of landscape become visible.

The progress is so gradual that one could wonder if it was not the eyes coming into focus, rather than the desert gaining definition.

Slowly the desert gathers form, revealing uncountable millions of years of tortuous complexity: weathered basalt and rock, eroded sandstone and dust; the sinuous pathways of deep arroyos; the canyons and cliffs with every shade of red, lilac, yellow, ochre and startling white, all telling their own stories.

And the small, knotted juniper everywhere, gnarled and twisted like ancient bonsai trees.

I am aware of birdsong, and the first hint of a morning breeze.

And now the sun squints over the mesa, and I have the first sight of its orb, rising swiftly now.

I turn my back on it.

Stretched out before me lies a starkly beautiful and unforgiving land; a desert virgin corrupted by light.

A weathered crone.

# HAIKU

Breathing the desert—
breathing the deep compassion—
of indifference

# TATTOO JESUS

*It was all about a picture from an old magazine*
*Jesus in the arms of Mary Magdalene*

Used to be a tattoo parlour going north on Guadeloupe
Artist there called Salvador come up from Mexico to Santa Fe
With his daughter who never spoke—and his wife the lovely Salome
That's where I got religion—one minute down from 285 Highway

It was a long hot summer—back in eighty-four
Cottonwoods just starting to turn when this big man comes through the door
Big man—come on a Harley—you could tell he's a loner
Said he'd been searching for Jesus all the way 'cross Arizona

A big man full of sadness—there was grief in his eye
Like something in his heart was dead—and something else didn't want to die
And he took out a picture torn from some magazine
Of Jesus with stigmata in the arms of Mary Magdalene

He took off his waistcoat—his chest was smooth as silk and bare
Handed them the torn print and said—"I want that tattooed here!"
And like a man nailed to a cross—he lay down with arms stretched out wide
And the pain on his face was of a man crucified

*It was all about a picture from an old magazine*
*Jesus in the arms of Mary Magdalene*


The sun had long set—the work glowed like a prayer
Salvador rose slowly from his working-chair
One broken hand lay soft upon the heart
And they waited in silence for the broken beat to start


*It was all about a picture from an old magazine*
*Jesus in the arms of Mary Magdalene*


Then—
Salvador's daughter spoke her first word ever—
The man raised himself—whole and free of the fever—
I saw—the passion of Jesus come alive—

And that's when I got religion—

# JACKRABBIT—RANCHO DE SAN JUAN

It is almost exactly twenty years since I saw the dead hare on the road.

I was on my way back from Laaiplek, a small village on the West Coast, not far from Saldanha Bay in southern Africa.

How many times since then have I imagined myself into her last few moments before she was struck by a passing vehicle?

Her death, and all my questions surrounding death, destiny, fate or seeming chance, the meaning or meaninglessness of life and what does or does not follow death, have occupied my mind these past two decades.

Today, in another country and under different circumstances, I have an answer. Not the kind of answer that can be understood rationally, but an answer, nevertheless.

We were staying at the Rancho de San Juan, a place on the Ojo Caliente road, just outside Española in northern New Mexico. The place is situated in one of the oldest deserts in the world, and the landscape spreads out all around in layers of dusky pink, blue heat haze and purple shadows.

It is a tortuous terrain, carved and weathered by sun, wind, snow and rain—and aeons of time.

New Mexico had just enjoyed some of the heaviest rains of the century, and the country was green, covered with juniper and piñon, tumbleweeds, wild sage and a wide variety of small flowering shrubs and grasses.

It was early morning, shortly after our arrival, before the sun moved over the mesa and the desert began to bake, when I started off up the arroyo, a dry riverbed close to where we were staying. I was aware that I was not familiar with the country or this terrain and did not know what I should watch out for other than scorpions and rattlesnakes, so I was mindful of this, and alert.

I was half-looking for stones, and I don't know what, when around a bend I spotted an almost perfect sphere of basalt. I bent down to pick it up and moved that critical inch too close to an unseen jackrabbit which was crouching under a tumbleweed, not two feet away from me.

The jackrabbit exploded out of the bush, and with great leaps took off up the side of the arroyo. Great, strong feet; long ears, flattened along his back; and tawny. In a few seconds he had vanished into the scrub and juniper.
I too had sprung back, and stood with my heart racing, adrenaline pumping. Transfixed.

Instantly, like two superimposed film images—transparencies—the two events, the dead hare on the road and this leaping jackrabbit, slide together—fuse. Death and life, in that moment, are one.

I have a sense of the brilliance of the sun; the dry earth, powdery like pink dust; the intense blue of the sky—and green.

I feel my smallness.

I feel the complete indifference of this land; more than that—the compassion of this indifference; as if the desert surrendered long ago, and has moved beyond all questions, beyond endurance, beyond any concept I can articulate; far beyond the considerations of life and death—into a timelessness.

The presence of the hare has answered the questions that I can barely form—a reply that cannot be spoken in any conventional way. But I am released from some tyranny of my rational mind.

I stand, blessed; the sun beating down on me; the dry twigs that I have gathered still clutched tightly in my hand.

And the stone I have found.

On the way back I saw him again, high above me on the rim of the arroyo. Another glimpse of his white tail, and he was gone.

Later, up at the house, I stood in the strong sunlight and took off all my clothes.

## A HUNTED ELK

A hunted elk—majestic horns
　　surrenders his life
　　a crown of thorns

## NUESTRA SEÑORA DE LOS TOROS

Beneath the spotless gown
a dark horn
—nudges—
a carnal and cloven rut
through fur and fragrant roses.

—"Bless me Father!"—

A bloodshot eye—
a taurine muzzle
nuzzles
its presence
—wetly—
into the submissive
Hail Marys.

# THE HOT SUMMER

It was a very hot summer.

It was so hot, that even the cactus that grew around the plaza withered that year.

It was so hot that the town's dogs, known for their cantankerous natures, lay silent and panting in the black pools of shadow cast by the adobe houses.

From time to time one or other would leave the pools of shade, purple as ripe plums, and lope across the small square to the water trough, there to lap the cool water, eyes closed against the heat and glare of the desert sand; only to return to the place of shade.

It was the summer of the marriage of Don Diego Fernandez to the beautiful Juanita.

An arranged marriage.

Don Diego was the collector of beautiful things, and the lovely Juanita was the latest addition to his possessions.
At fifty-one, Don Diego was thirty-two years older than his bride, who was said to be the most beautiful woman ever to set foot in that town.

It was the summer—the hot summer—when three things happened in the small town.

Many people said it was all on account of the heat.

Some disagreed.

Be that as it may, it was because of the heat that Don Diego decided to visit his cousin in the cooler foothills, leaving his new, young bride alone in the big house with the servants.

It was because of the heat that Juanita, dressed only in a soft, white cotton shift, sat in the doorway of the big house, which opened onto the square—sat brushing her long, black hair that was as straight and shiny and sleek as the night wind—brushing with long, slow, languid strokes, over and over, to comfort the loneliness that ached in her heart.

It was because of the heat that the young boy, Juan Hermoso Fuentes, was sent to fill a pail of water from the trough in the square, for his mother's kitchen.

The boy, Juan, was tall for his age. His features were pure Castilian. He had a flawless, olive skin, black hair that fell, straight and silent, to his shoulders; eyes that burned with darkness.

As he passed the big house, he felt drawn to look over the low adobe wall.

It was the small movement in the shade of the doorway that caught his attention.

It was then that his eyes met those of the beautiful, young woman seated in the doorway.

It was then—in that instant—that his future, and his fate, were sealed.

# MRS FERNANDEZ

*Mrs Fernandez—Mrs Fernandez*
*I carry your love inside of me*
*I've tasted the black wind*
*I've tasted the shadow*
*This heart of mine will never be free*

I fell in love with Mrs Fernandez
Fell out of my boyhood when I was thirteen
Stole my first kiss
Drank my first brandy
Lay naked as heaven with a dark Magdalene

I fell in love with Mrs Fernandez
The scent of her body—black wind in her hair
The curve of her breast
The heat and the fever
The passions of love that linger there

*Mrs Fernandez—Mrs Fernandez*
*I carry your love inside of me*
*I've tasted the black wind*
*I've tasted the shadow*
*This heart of mine will never be free*

Now I'm a man—women are many
In every town—a fresh beauty queen
But where is the black wind?
Where is the fever?
Where is the fire of my dark Magdalene?

*Mrs Fernandez—Mrs Fernandez*
*I carry your love inside of me*
*I've tasted the black wind*
*I've tasted the shadow*
*This heart of mine will never be free*

# DESERT MOON

Moon over Black Mesa
and an infinity of stars—

now—
coyotes weave their voices
on the warp of desert air—

And now—
this stillness
this impossible moon—

## HAIKU

Black mesa turned white—
overnight—while we slept on—
snow fell—winter light—

## HAIKU

Mist rising slowly—
ghost mesas drift in convoy
across the white plains—

## HAIKU

Shed your skins—your clothes!
Lose the name you were given!
Only nakedness!

# TRES PIEDRAS
New Mexico

The Ojo Caliente road up to Tres Piedras climbs steadily from New Mexico's Chama River valley, with its smattering of doublewides and prefab houses, its smallholdings and the occasional café, to a vast plain approximately 2 000 meters above sea level. Here three stark outcroppings of brown sandstone, the only feature in the landscape, give the place its name—Tres Piedras, Three Rocks.

There is a point in the journey when you realise that you are no longer looking up at the dark mesa, but down over the valley and the desert. With the increase in elevation, the vegetation changes from green valley through sparse dry land, dotted with juniper, piñon and sage bush, to forest—the Carson National Forest.

The road through Ojo Caliente is a minor road with little traffic, apart from the transport vehicles. These, huge and predatory in appearance, resemble giant, shiny locusts with diesel smokestacks like silver antennae, which puff out black diesel smoke as they thunder past on their thirty and sometimes forty wheels.

Tres Piedras is a bleak place. It is not yet autumn, but the sky is overcast, the clouds low and oppressive. A cold wind, which in winter drives the blizzards that often cut off Tres Piedras from the world, seems to cut right through my clothing. The stunted juniper and piñon bushes look almost black.

Held within the narrow strip between earth and sky, a flat plain extends monotonously into a nondescript blur, and would appear to end only at some distant mountains. Silver green sage bush is the most noticeable vegetation.

The main drag boasts a fire station, a grocery store and café, a gas station, a few houses and a derelict building which I see from the writing on the roof was once the Chamber of Commerce, but now appears to be a liquor outlet.

The buildings are drab and faded and have not seen paint in a long while. In contrast to these, on the other side of the road and some distance from the others, a conspicuously pink building called the School House, which doubles as a gallery, stands incongruous and self-conscious under a new coat of paint. It would appear to be the pride of Tres Piedras.

A sign on the roadside says—"Stop for a Bone of your Own."

I pull over. A tall man—tanned dark from the sun, shabbily dressed in blue jeans, shirt and leather waistcoat; hair, beard, moustache all grizzled and unkempt—strolls over to me. He could be anywhere between thirty-five and sixty years.

"Yer lookin' f'r a bone?"

I am aware of my tidiness.

I tell him I just came over to see what he has. He shows me the bones—a sad collection of bits of weathered bone: a cow's sacrum, part of a goat's skull with one horn, a dog skull—only the upper jaw, a coyote skull and some small bits and pieces which could be almost anything. His main attraction is a box supporting two sticks with eagle skulls attached to them, bound on with wire and leather and sporting tassels of elk-hide.

On a makeshift table, he has a tired collection of faded leatherware that looks as if it has been lying in the sun for years. Trade does not appear to be brisk in Tres Piedras.

"Made it m'self." He shows me the stitching and threadbare lining.

I settle for a small pouch, unlined, made of elk-skin, and a leather wristband with five Buffalo Dimes on it. "We don' 'av' this currency no mor.'"

He tells me he moved up from the city seven years ago; lives here with his horse and his donkey.

"Folk don' trouble me none."

I ask him where he lives, and he gestures over his shoulder into what looks like open space. I see nothing.

"Yeah—ah' live there—don' cos' me nuttin'. Here ah kin ride ma hosse when ah chews. Ah hav' t'charge f'r the bones 'cos' ma hosse, he don' work f'r nuttin'. Mind—he can graze all summer—but ah help him out in th' win'er."

When I drive off, about half a mile down the road, I see a small shack with a lean-to and a fence of weathered sticks, all blown over to one side. The shack is scarcely bigger than a packing case and seems to be largely propped up by an assortment of boxes, a metal barrel and bits and pieces of junk. It would seem to offer little protection in a fierce storm. If this is his dwelling, it must be hard living in the winter.

I find myself wondering what his future will be, and what will happen to him when he is old or sick. Suppose he falls off his horse—breaks a leg. Would anyone miss him? Does he have any friends? What does he live on? Surely not the takings of his stall and the bones? Would anyone even know if he died? Or care?

I consider my life with all its demands, relationships and complexities: my busyness, all my attachments, ambitions, hopes, fears, doubts. The list is endless. Has he really managed to let go of all of it? Is it really possible to live so lightly on the land? Or is this just grinding poverty? Is his dropping out a giving up, and let the devil take the end of it?

Or, perhaps, salvation?

I will never know the end of his story.
I drive home, my thoughts full of him. Was his choice courageous? Or an easy way out?
Whichever it was, "Ah guess it don' trouble him none."

## MILAGRO

Today there is no wind—
I listen to the resonance of your voice
—your song—
and hear it fly out across this silent land
a desert hawk
—dark—
against the desert sky
and watch it
—skim—
the long—long sweeping curve—
of a soft horizon's rim.

Today there is no wind
—the sky is full of blue—

and I listen to the desert
—breathing in—
the resonance of this song
—breathed out by you—
a lifetime ago
and on a distant shore

yet echoes here
—in silent rock—
and the mesa's shadowed fall

and in my heart
—a resonance—
evermore.

Today there is no wind
—the sky is full of blue—
and I am breathing you.

# THE ARROYO

The path that I am on leads nowhere.

Walking the bones of this dry arroyo
—the air dense with heat—
the light
—tangible as the pungent scent of juniper—
vibrates
with green and sky
and I
—stripped of all clothing—
know I am alive.

Naked
I follow my feet
—leading me where they will—
as if permission to obey some older law were granted me.

My hands gather in treasure upon treasure
—pebbles—fragments of quartz—and basalt—
strange shapes of wood
—curled and weathered—
and pieces of bone.

I follow
where I am led
—breathing in deep this high thin air—
feeling the desert
holding me
releasing me

and deep within
—my rooted song—
so old
so new

—and I—
touched by the light
—this light that sings through me—
filling me
—so that I am drunk with it—
know
that I am young again.

One more turn
—one gentle curve and wide—
and a woman
—a weathered crone—
her hands—thin—blue-veined
with papery skin
—holding pebbles and bent twigs and stone—
is at my side.

Something familiar about the way she stands.
Something in the turn of her head
—a certain look—
—the expression in her eyes—
that I remember
—half-remember—
as if we'd met once.

Or perhaps the way she moves her hand up to her hair
—I seem to know—
almost recognise.

We walk on in light and silence
—she and I—
on down the bones of this deep arroyo
—step for step—
on into the distance—
—she bending down with me when I bend down—
reaching for rock or stick
or bone—

pausing with me when I pause
turning with me when I turn.
And so we went on.

But it was then
—when the path vanished—
and she turned her crone's face toward me
—it was then—
I knew it for my own.

# DRIFTWOOD

I have fallen in love with the world.

Today, in the arroyo, I found—of all unlikely things—a piece of weathered wood: worn smooth, like driftwood, scarcely bigger than two fingers, but delicate, its centre sculpted into gentle shapes, and hollow spaces by some agency. I couldn't miss it—even in the arroyo's shadow—for it appeared to be lit from within.

I don't know how long I sat, holding it in my open hand.

Finally, when I examined it closely, I saw that it probably originated as a piece of wood that had been cut and planed, possibly in a factory—a rather well-defined right-angle suggests this.

It might have been used in a building, or perhaps in a piece of furniture. At some stage in its life, a woodworm may have lived in it; some tunnel-like grooves show signs of this.

How long has it lain in the desert, weathering; and how did it come to be in the arroyo at all? And then, by what chance did I find it, wedged between two pieces of basalt?

I have looked up "driftwood" in a dictionary. One meaning of "drift" comes from the older root "drive", the way cattle are driven, or the way a piece of wood has been driven, by wind or water.

I marvel at the possible scope of its history. It has allowed—what cannot be resisted.

It rests in the palm of my hand: the messenger, and the message. Can I hear it?

It appears to me to be a figure—part human, perhaps part animal. It could be many things.

It has a smallish head, on a long, slender neck, a strangely formed body, a primitive figure which appears to be carrying some kind of burden. My mind goes to a photograph, in a book I have, of San Bushmen in southern Africa. I am going to assume she is female, because of the bundle she is carrying.

She has a huge presence.

I imagine her thirty feet high mounted in open desert, where she can be seen for miles around. Her impact on a viewer would be great enough to stop the mind. In my mind—in another reality—she is already there.

Would the desert creatures recognise her—be drawn to her—this strange, new form, standing up so tall in their landscape? Would they, too, feel the numinous power of her presence?

I am going to mount her on a piece of wood, like a miniature sculpture.

I allow my imagination to follow a path I cannot see. I wait. And then they come—images.

A deeper story: that in spite of being a tree, and then a piece of wood, and then a discarded piece of something else—something no one wants, no one sees, for how many years until now—that still she is.

Are we, like her, already the next chapter in a vast story?

What is this figure to me? And what am I to her? What then is this commanding presence?
If only I could hear her voice.

I am waiting. Listening. Will I understand her speech?

At first, I hear only the sound of the wind. But now—listen! Wind has no sound of its own. It must be given by something else. Yes—I can hear the wind in a forest—a vast forest that knows mountains and mountain mist. And snow.

And then the images speak to me; all at once. How do I explain that I see a thousand images—simultaneously? That this figure was once a tree, among many thousands, in a forest. Undifferentiated.

But then it was felled; separated from its roots, and all the years of its growing. It spent long years drifting down a river. It was loaded, transported, cut into long planks, leaving little sign of its original form; stacked, stored—waiting to be sold.

The images come like a rush of wind. There is no time, no sequence in this vision.

Who can ever tell the full story of that life?

Of any life?

Yet still she is!

"Will you tell me your story?" I whisper. "How you come to be here in this arroyo?"

When she answers, her voice is soft. Only a trace of sound. Am I imagining this? They are not words.

"I can say only that I am."

I lean closer. I have never heard such ancient speech; yet I can understand it.

"You cannot destroy me. Knowing this, I am peaceful."

I can feel the beginning of tears. Who is this? I feel as if I stand on hallowed ground.

"I have been many things—and always I am what I always was. "You can burn me—I will be in the smoke, and in the fragrance that drifts over the land.

"Grind me into dust—I will find rest in the earth, and my soul will be part of some new growth."

I find that I am on my knees, holding this small form in both my cupped hands, and letting my tears fall. All around me, the world is still. Only this soft breath of wind.

"For this instant of time, I am a small figure in the palm of your hand, and this is our meeting."

I know there is more. I wait.

"But our story has no beginning that can be told—nor any end."

The faint trace of air is growing softer. I lean forward to hear—

I want to say—"Don't leave me—"

—The inner light is fading—

"You and I are One."

—A trace of air

"—One Breath—"

## HAIKU
*for Larry Schwartz*

Forget about time.
The illusion of distance.
Here and now—we meet.

## HAIKU
*for Larry Schwartz*

Across the no-time—
echoes of the oud's soft strings
transform the silence—

## ON THE ROAD TO TAOS

Today
I saw the shadows cut an epitaph into the long low desert hills
—and etch with hard light—
the stark and crumpled edges of their imperishable beauty.

Those broken hills
distant and full of secrets
bare of all cover
and eroded by centuries of storms.

I knew then that I was saying goodbye—
that I would not come this way again.

And suddenly—
the whole land
—leaped—
into immediate attention
—and all that magnificent remoteness fell away—

and I saw
—that this sense of loss—
was not mine alone.

Everything longs to be seen.

## DESERT—NEW MEXICO

I cannot find the words to describe the overwhelming beauty
—the vast dimensions—
and the ever-changing moods
of this land.

There is something unfathomable about this desert
—which even as I attempt to know it—
recedes into depths of antiquity that forbid all entry.

No words
that I ascribe to it
will suffice.

How dare I try to hold
in words
—that which is forever changing—
even as it remains changeless?

Perhaps later—on reflection
—when the land and all its attributes are absent—
perhaps then—
I will be able to distil from memory
something of its essence.

But for now—I am at a loss.

How to describe that moment that comes towards evening
—that moment—
when the distinction between

        colour—
        light—
       and form—
     disappears?

How to put into words
the sure knowledge
—that the souls of the dead—
who have lived here for thousands of years
—are tangibly present—
in the earth—
the hills—
the sky?

How to describe
that dark illumination
—on a moonless night—
that numinous
penumbral
light

—that comes from millions—upon millions of stars—

and reveals the darkness
to itself?

# HAIKU

This infinite sky—
this dark night of countless stars—
this empty silence—

# RANCHO DE SAN JUAN

A clear day when we left. A few clouds in an immense sky.

I said goodbye to the small adobe casita—to all the funny little treasures: the five-dollar hare with twigs of juniper on its back, the stone hawk, all the small Zuni fetishes, and the elk horn from the trading store in Chama, the pebbles I had gathered with my granddaughter.
Said goodbye to the whole story of love—and its attendant shadow—which gathers soul and substance in a place much loved.

There is a time—just when it first comes, I am not sure—but a time when you realise that a goodbye may be forever. I may never see this small desert house again: never again look out at the stark mesa, the sandstone cliffs, the dark, brooding falls of scree.

May never again stand under this vast, blue dome of sky and watch the jet planes from Los Alamos draw those long, white lines that melt into infinity in the sky; never again look out at the flat horizontals of the distant mesas, with all around me that grand, sweeping curvature of the land, falling down the horizon; may never again stand out on a warm night, under an impossible desert moon, listening to the singing of the coyotes.

Now, standing here, saying farewell—my feet bare, feeling the powdery texture of the earth, the sun burning into me although it is still early morning, I realise that there is a solitude that I will never leave; can never lose—a voice that, all unawares, has imprinted itself into my soul.

# HAIKU

Blue sky—blue mountains.
All one thing—where does it end?
Where do I begin?

# DUENDE

Beneath this vast sky everything is small
—the desert unforgiving—
and this dark wind!

To wrestle a poem
—from such uncompromising gods—
is to risk everything.

## Through My Window

Through my window
the desert rainstorm paints
a water-colour landscape

## A Still World of Mist and Rain

A still world of mist and rain—
and the pale lost ghosts
of the crumpled hills

## After the Rain

After the rain—
a juniper alight
with a fire of hummingbirds

## ONE DAY

One day
you have the dream

that has dreamed you
a thousand times

that will dream you forever

though you deny it in your forgetting
though you turn away to other things.

But one day
you awaken

you leave the dream

you step into your new life

hearing a voice
that you have always known

the one who has loved you
since before the day you were born.

# THE SILENCE OF SALT

First—
I must tell you of my origins
that I am of stone
breath of wolf
shape of leaf
—and wind—
wing of bird.

I must speak to you of strangeness.

And I must speak of that place where the wind sleeps
and of wild things
—the silence of animals—
—the silence of footprints—
and the scent of their silence.

I first learnt this strangeness as an orphan
—listening to the night—
—listening to a child's terror—
and the immense night outside my window.

This was when I first heard the wolf howl.
This was the start of my initiation.
I had not yet come to the silence of salt.

It has taken a lifetime to hear what moves beyond the world
—to cleanse myself of all other learning—
to listen into the absence of sound

and hear

—that soundless note the world makes—
as it turns
around and around the silent curve of space.

I once heard a singing in the eye of a fish
—just before it died—
a song of wonderment—

and when I first became a woman
—I heard the lament of the moon—
its longing for water.

I knew then that I would give my life to it.
Would learn to walk
—if only once—
upon its mystery.

But it is the silence of salt that calls me now
this deep strangeness
—with its memory of sea—
a cautery—
a memory—
that burns like fire.

# SOLITUDE

Everyone must leave home
—eventually—
if only at their death.

It is only one step—
and we spend a lifetime
taking it.

Yet see how gracefully
the blossom falls—
how autumn drops its leaves
without regret—
how animals turn to their fate
with more composure
—in their innocence—
than I can muster
with all of my reason.

The days draw in.
I feel their solitude.

It is not comfort I require now—
nor all the teachings of the world.

It is not some articulated faith I need—
but
innocence.

# THIS CHANGING FACE

This ragged voice that struggles to become
This song of longing that is the best of me
Will not be silenced though the walls grow high
So high
And only a memory of blue remains where once was sky

This landscape which is my longing
This solitude—my only prayer
And the young lover always out of reach
Somewhere above me on the winding stair

This voice inside of me has burned a thousand times
Too small it feels for all its memories
How strange it seems to own this changing face
This trembling earth beneath my feet
This once bright and hallowed place

This landscape which is my longing
This solitude—my only prayer
And the young lover always out of reach
Somewhere above me on the winding stair

# THE RIVER PEOPLE

I am following the footprints of a dream.
I am following a dream
—that lies beneath a river—
—somewhere in a red-earth desert—
and beyond the sky.

I am called to this place of solitude
—this land of silences—
to walk this blood-landscape
—summoned
by a threefold shape-shift presence
—that melts and merges with the mirage—
that walks upon the shining and elusive waters
of this desert Galilee.

I am called by their faceless lament
—this deep imperative—
this high-pitched ululation
this keening howl of song.

You think that I am mad?
My father would know otherwise.

For I am listening to a deeper vein of truth
—deeper than any I have found—
in this webbed world of information.

I am listening to the deep and silent language of a dream.
A song sung in images.
A deep and silent river song.

# GOATS AND THORN TREES

There's a river beneath the river
Sings a hidden song
And the white goats eat the thorn trees
All day long

Red sand—blue sky
Sing a desert song
And the white goats eat the thorn trees
All day long

All day long—
All day long—
All day long—
All day long—

Where does the wind go?
Where does the wind belong?
And the white goats eat the thorn trees
All day long

There's a naked boy weaves a hat
Sings a goatherd song
And the white goats eat the thorn trees—

## THE WAY SALT LONGS FOR THE SEA

I am a lover of silence—
a lover of solitude—
and the taste of salt.

I am called now to the silence of this mountain
this high, thin place
—that sings into the very blood of me—
to feel as I climb—in the narrow windings of my soul—the world fall
away—

feel the soft pelt start to form over my body
from within—
feel the guard-hairs—rise—and—prick—
like stealthy footprints
down the keen ridge of my spine
and the newly fleshed animal of my body
muscle out—alive—electric
with the immediacy of sharp attention
—and all my senses alert—
to the scent and sound of wild.

I am called to this silence the way salt longs for the sea
—the way it burns a path through rock and mountain and desert sand—
—a pilgrimage—
that leaves a stinging residue
—a covenant—
of sacred and bitter on the land.

I long for this silence to cauterise me of all conceit.

To shrive my soul of all complexity.

And leave me
—as still and silent—

as a ring of vapour around the moon.

# THE SONG OF THE RED EARTH

Forever I have lain with you in red earth—
before ever time was
—I knew you—
naked as the wind I have held you
—held your soul—
close
to my naked breast.

From moonlight I have sculpted your form
in the image of my desire
the lithe and supple length of you
like a bow
—slender as an arrow—
your body
simple as a flower.

I have dreamed you out of the stars—
out of the blue fire of heaven.

My senses burn at the sight of your beauty—
my touch calls forth the sultry night
so full of heat
—a blood moon rising—
and your body aching over me
wanting me
wanting me with the heat of your longing
wanting to lose itself forever in me
aching with longing to enter me
to fill me

wanting to die in me
again
and again
and again.

I come to you Beloved
forever a virgin.
Hear me.

\*

I want to tell you how beautiful you are—
I want to touch you
move you
undo you

I want to enter you
take you so tenderly
and print my soul upon your soul

I want to know that wildness
that breathes
behind the shadows in your eyes

I want to see your naked face

\*

Touch me
taste me
breathe me into your soul

cover me
corrupt me
this immaculate flame

Take me now
—wound me—
undo me with your eyes
—suffer me—
—save me—
this unconsummated flame

# SOUL

Where did we lose that untamed animal we once called soul
—that used to run wild beyond imagination—
blow through the landscape of our dreams
or drift through great washes of sleep and shadows
—large and silent as whales—
or lie etched with blood and memory in earth's striations?
It seems so far away.

Once we cast our nets
—for the sheer joy of it—and fearing nothing—
into those primordial tides
—lay beneath stars—
our souls reflected in the sultry moon for our contemplation.

It was a country so vast
so full of wonder
—innocent of all explanation—
that our childhood eyes—half-closed and dazzled—
would gaze upon it in simple bliss—
a world now written over with sophistication
—complex and comfortless—
and scribed in certainty with proof by science—
or bound about by "thou shalt not" and such.

Where now the animal that was us?
Where now that mettle—that fierce rage—the fine fettle of youth's blood
—that coursed like fire behind our eyes
—that knew itself to be invincible—
Where now the dream to end all dreams?

It seems that long before we have the eyes to see it
—before we learn to read that smaller print—
we will betray it
—betray that savage innocence—that free un-tempered wind.
So be it.
Now let them speak of heresy.

Let them send their missionaries with flags unfurled.
I will tear up all contracts that bind me to their small and shrinking world—
will fight to be this once and only creature
—this unique and solitary me—
this being that is cast—by life—or destiny—or by what mystery—I never shall understand
—into this breathless universe
—this shining land.

# NAKED

I want to live my life in that fierce flame that lights the eagle's stare.
Open my heart to the wild cat's scream.
Fall to the dark earth like a star.
Offer all that I am to the cutting flint of crucifixion.

I want to run naked as desire over dark hills
and drown in starry nights of wonder.

I want to breathe this splendid rage
—into my blood—
—into my bones—
into the haunting seas of memory.

I want to swim the slow thinking of fish
—and feel the world stream through me—
its huge unstoppable tides.

I want to walk beneath the raging branches of the storm
—hear the rattle of bones lost to the wind—
I want to cleave the sky like a hawk's wing
and blow away
like dust—
or ash—
or forgetting.

I want to live at the cutting edge of myself
—with the presence of grinning death perched upon my shoulder—
—whispering—
—always whispering—

I want to learn his dark song.
I want to sing it to the wind.
I want to walk on water.

# THE CREATION

From the salt floor of the desert he gathered a rattle of bones—
and forged the mettle of his armature—
fashioned the vital form
out of dust from a storm of stars.

He cut a stealthy pelt
from the shadows of the silver thorn—
and fixed the mystery of the moon into the orbit of his eyes.

He blew the breath of wild into his nostrils—
cut claws from the flint-edges of the earth—
and into his throat he strung the high and lonely howl of the north-west wind.

And he set the silence of night upon his footprints.

He took from the sea her tireless rhythm
—sang it into the long loping length of him—

—ran a shiver of lightning down the lupine curve of the supple spine—

and lit the halo of raised guard-hairs
with the scent of danger.
And he fastened him with rage—
and he set fierce rivers of fire coursing to every nerve and fibre—
at his command.

Into his heart he placed the thunder of the gods—
and he burned into his blood and brain the indelible brand of wild.

         And then—
    —blinded by such beauty—
     he fell beside the river—

and out of a clod of sullen clay

            he fashioned
             the first
              man.

# ODE TO MYSTERY

What mystery then—
when all the measurements are done?
I pray the gods may scuttle all conclusions.

I can hold it in my hands
—this skull—
—this house of heaven and hell—
this ivory cave made old with wind and shadows—
where images make play upon her walls—
and memory cradles her haunting song.

A work of centuries—
this box of whisperings and numinous emanations—
this hermetic cell
—of finite measure—
yet holds an inner sky
—wider than ever I could dream it—
infinity—vast—boundless—
and terrifying.

This domed vessel of knitted bone resounds
with intuitions—and superstitions
—and dark penumbral imaginings
—and evil
—and innocence
—and small satisfactions
—and greatness

and deep within the flower and fruit—
the root of instinct.

All the seasons of the soul are gathered here—
and histories we have not yet recalled.
And longing—
and desire—
and death—
and madness—

and a fierce black wind to blow the night sky full of stars and mystery.

The beating of my heart brings metre and measure to it.

And you are here.
And I.
And all eternity blowing through it.

# THE DAWNING OF THE DARK

I am called to kneel
This is the dawning of the dark
I am called to kneel
In this beautiful dark prayer
My hands are empty
I can hear the thunder
The Holy Dove's on my shoulder
Dark is dawning everywhere

My heart is full—my hands are empty
All around me this dark dark prayer
The Holy Dove is on my shoulder
Dark is dawning everywhere

I am called to kneel
Beside the hidden river
I am called to kneel
Heart and soul on fire
Earth and heaven are one
The Holy Dove's on my shoulder
Day and night are cast
Into an ancient gyre

My heart is full—my hands are empty
All around me this dark dark prayer
The Holy Dove is on my shoulder
Dark is dawning everywhere

## THE RAVEN'S CALL

I heard the raven call.
And I heard the sound of weeping.
And I heard the unsung dead
cry out—
in their unremembered sleeping.

And I felt the shaking earth
—open—
and fall away from me—
and I saw the raven light upon a many-branching tree—

and I heard the voice of heaven
—thunder—
—calling out to me—
to go down to the dead lands
and set the dead men free.

And again—
the voice of heaven
sounded
—from deep within my breast—

"Go down"—it said—"to the dead lands—
and bring the dead men rest."

And I walked among those shadows—
and the haunting undead cries—
where the captive dead lay waiting
for someone

—just to close their eyes—

and I felt my hands reach out
—and touch—
each broken soul

—one by one—

and say a prayer and close those eyes—
that their waiting may be done.

I heard the raven call from the land of the dead
where the unsung men lay sleeping
with no stone beside their head.

## SANTA FE NEW MEXICO

A heavy snowfall overnight.
It is late afternoon.
Turning left into Santa Fe off the 287, under a blazing sunset sky, she sees the raven flying low over the white hill, and over all the small, white gravestones.

Many of these graves mark the burial places of men from New Mexico who died in the Vietnam War.

## THE WEEPING

A raven flying over snow
A shadow raven lost below
Nothing moves—all is still
But the sound of weeping

A song of sorrow in my head
A cold lament for the unsung dead
No one listens—nobody hears
The sound of weeping

So go to the shadow
Turn your back to the sun
I won't be back
Till the song is sung
I won't be back
Till the weeping's done

A raven flying over snow
A shadow raven lost below
A sound of grief—a song unsung
I won't be back—till the weeping's done

No I won't be through with weeping—no
And the dead
And the dead
And the dead will never sleep—

And the raven will fly—

# THE SUDDEN COMING

It is the sudden coming of the tide
and a voice calling.

It is the waves capsized
and time shaking.

It is the sweet ache climbing
in unbearable beauty.

It is my own deep knowing
naked in my hands.

It is all the days that I am—and that I shall be—

exploding in a burst of light.

It is the flesh delivered—

and the Spirit

still—

# INHERITANCE

It is not a dream—
this pain that has no voice—
this landscape of unnamed sorrows.

And always—this haunting wind
—this sleek and shining blackness—
this place of strange visitation.

No one enters this dark wind
but is made silent by the watching night
and empty of all longing.

And will find here
—only the absence of things—
the absence of voice
and touch
and tears.

Will find here—
a place made hollow by hunger.
What else but pain could bear such emptiness?

And yet—
it is in this abandoned place
—this raven night of wounds and sorrows—
that she stands
—the howled-thin feral child—

the inheritor of such
fierce
wild
beauty.

## SHALL I FOLLOW YOU?

Shall I follow you
through that dark landscape
of wounds and sorrows

even to the origins of pain
and betrayal—

and discover—
how grief opens up a doorway in the soul—
and lays before us lands we never dared to dream were true?

# This Darkness Obscures All Vision

This darkness obscures all vision.
One small candle—lit—
will undo it.

# THIS FLAME

Now—only my intuition remains.
This last call to mission.

I am
stretched out on the dark earth
and staked—like a cow-hide—thin almost to breaking.

Crucified upon the cross of reason—
and the deep well of vision.

I am drawn into this dark mystery
—this unholy flame—
drawn or driven
by my hunger

just once to know your face—
just once to hear my name.

# THIS DARK AND LOVELY WOUND

You are a storm in my heart
That breaks and breaks like a tide in me
A fierce and startling sorrow
Inside of me

And the taste of salt on the wind
Night-tide calling
Sea-mist rolling in
Night falling

I hear your name in every forest wind
A wild song in the heart of me
Suffer this dark and lovely wound
So much a part of me

And the taste of salt on the wind
Night-tide calling
Sea-mist rolling in
Night falling

# WHAT IS OUR WOUNDING?

What is our wounding
if not desire?
And the Blood Moon calls us.

And what is our longing
if not our blood?
And the Blood Moon calls us.

And what is our blood
but that it spills to kiss the rim of our dark wounding?

And the Blood Moon calls us.
And the Blood Moon ever calls us.

And how may we call forth the courtship of earth and blood—
except we enter that dark wound—
except we enter the dark earth—
except the Blood Moon calls us?

Or sing the forest into being—
or draw the moon from out the mountain—
or cast our souls to the black wind—
except the Blood Moon calls us?
And the Blood Moon ever calls us.

Or kiss the mounting tide that pulls the earth apart
—and throw away all measure—
except we lose ourselves in that other death—
except we lose ourselves?

What is our wounding
if not desire?

And the Blood Moon calls us.

# THE UNVEILING

The black earth burns beneath my feet.
There is no place that is not consumed.
The holy bush lifts its flames to the heavens—
and the sky is empty of tears.

How may I walk in such a land—
where the white fire brands my soul—
where the brutal uncovering of desire
—wounds me—
even to the bone?

## DARK RADIANCE

The cry of this child calls me to a naked shore—
returns me to a place that is empty of footprints.

Again and again
I come to this place—
looking for the child
dressed in blue.

There is beauty
in this dark emptiness
these black and shadowed
caverns of soul.

And now—
a raven moon
calls up a tide of old bones
to rattle into song the broken fragments of memory.

# GRAVID

Tonight—there is a black hand on the moon—and the sky is stained with blood.

Listen—
do you hear the wind's lament?
It is weeping for the child of blood and sorrows.

Tonight there is a black hand on my heart—
and a wound that does not heal.
What is the nature of this grief
that will not leave me?

Tonight there is a stain of blood in the sky—and a song of begetting.

What midwife hand is it now summons this birth?
What blood-child is it now struggles to be born?

# HAIKU

Learning is easy—
it is the long unlearning
that is so painful

# LOOKING BACK

Looking back now—
I see the long road stretching out behind—
far more behind—than ever lies ahead
nor would I try to plan the measure
of its future windings—

would no longer dare ask
how long a long road reaches—
or predict the nature of its course—
or plan a destination.

As for darkness—
I have not been afraid to fall.
But some wells—it seems—are too deep to fathom—
some shadows—too dark to know the light.

A far greater hand than mine is writing me.
An ancient hand—that scrawls the blueprint fate has cast my way—
characters in some script—unreadable to me.

Older than knowledge—far older than history.

Not much—it seems
—have I learnt in all this time—
for I have left youth and its certainty
far behind.

And most of what I thought I knew—
turns out to be irrelevant.

Yet—
one thing
—wonder—
—has endured the test—
and that saves the rest.

# COMING HOME

coming in from the sea
coming home now
coming to this country
coming home to this place
where my soul
once asleep in its forgetting
dreamed this place
out of the bones of memory

coming in from the sea
coming now to this land
from the bones of my forgetting
coming home
my body aching
with the memory of it
and yearning
my soul
once asleep in its forgetting
now returning to this place.

behind me that dark sea
the dark nights of my soul
behind me
the dark place of my crossing
the darkness of my forgetting.

behind me, there,
in that darkness
an unexpected compassion

and something approaching tenderness
almost intimacy
there—in that darkness
that place of suffering
and slow remembering
and deep remorse

there—the blessing of tears
absolution granted
in those dark waters

coming in from the sea now
from the dark sea
coming home
coming home
returning
to the country of my forgetting
to the country of my soul

coming in from the sea
coming home

# SONG FOR LYNDALL

Rattle of a wagon on the dirt road
Smell of dust before the rain
Sound of distant thunder
Sound of coming home again

This landscape is my homecoming
Dirt road melts into the sky
Open space and soft horizon
Fill the eye

*Karoo—Karoo I'm coming*
*A song of dying in my brain*
*Karoo—Karoo I'm coming*
*Coming home again*

Sun on the koppies and the sound of thunder
Dust in my nostrils and the smell of rain
Landscape and its thirst for colour
And endless plain

*Karoo—Karoo I'm coming*
*A song of dying in my brain*
*Karoo—Karoo I'm coming*
*Coming home again*

## LET ME LIE DOWN AND DRINK THE WIND

My soul does not want to leave this house
This sacred place of blood and bone
This country of many gatherings
Salt and wind-blown

My soul does not want to leave this house
With all its slow seasons of heart and mind
With all its solitude and silence
Naked in the wind

*But now the sky is in my footprints*
*And the river runs beneath the sand*
*My feet are bare—my heart is naked*
*Let me lie down and drink the wind*

This is my house of moths and butterflies
A house of stories at the edge of my mind
A place of memory and forgetting
Let me lie down and drink the wind

*And now the sky is in my footprints*
*And the river runs beneath the sand*
*My feet are bare—my heart is naked*
*Let me lie down and drink the wind*

# FISH I

beneath the waves where spirals meet
and silent centuries await—
a thought is thinking
—slow as fish—
that haunt the shadowed caverns there—

and slow as fish
from sullen depths
gleams the light on silver scale—

an eye evolves within the spiral
the thought explodes within the eye

and mute and scale
in primal reaches—
still hid
the aching knowledge lies

# FISH II

I see the first fish taking form
who rising from the primal darkness finds
—on scaly wings and from the deep un-focus—
the sudden stabbing gasp of spirit breath

I see a great stone rising
on the wings of the wind
and I with it

# FISH III

beautiful fish
with the moon in your belly
flying through the night sky
on scaly wings

I am waiting—
I am waiting—
on the rooftops of my mind
lying on the rooftops of the sleeping town—

come my lunar lover
let my arms embrace you
no colder than your body is my heart of stone

let me fly away with you
through the gaping maw of night
let me drown in your eyes
before the dawn

# FISH IV

a flying fish from the deeps he came
I saw him gasp the spirit breath
and cleave the wind
and arc the light

fin and scale
I saw him fall
back to the depths
from whence he came

but I saw you fish
I saw you fly
in that leap of time when our eyes met
and your fiery eye—so terrified with beauty
held my own—
I saw you—and we spoke

—I know you fish—

before he fell
his eye glazed and he died

# FISH V

oh radiant and enlightened fish
how fit it is that you should know
you the oldest of all living things
—how long have you dwelt in the darkness and the half-light—

and now you have leapt up
to swallow the sun

# EARLY MORNING

Only the ridge of the mountain

is lit

the sky is leaden

the ring of white stones in the garden

waits

and the doves in the trees

## TILL ALL YOUR WATERS GO OVER ME

I will not go down from this mountain
Till I feel your hand on me
I will not go down from this high mountain
Until you bless me
I will not go down into the darkness waiting
I will not go down
Till all your waters go over me

What is this world with all its hungers?
What is a river that never finds the sea?
What am I except I surrender
To the darkness inside of me?

I will not go down from this mountain
Till I feel your hand on me
I will not go down from this high mountain
Until you bless me
I will not go down into the darkness waiting
I will not go down
Till all your waters go over me

## STONE COTTAGE: WEST COAST
*for Di Steward*

The silence in this stone cottage
is as old as the cave.

In the rough hearth
—white-wash and burnt clay—
a fire awakens
a primitive connection.

Outside—
everything bends to the rain.

The night is cold.

And the darkness cannot find us.

## THIS SMALL ROOM

This small room is so full of stillness—

I can hear the beating of a thousand hearts.

The sound of a thousand songs.

Can hear the music of their solitude.

Can hear the wind speak outside my window.

Can hear the ecstatic chanting of this once and always mystery—

inside
my heart.

## HAIKU
*for Sherry Woods*
*in praise of spacing and format.*

For each dot and dash
—that comes between the telling—
offer a prayer.


## HAIKU

So obsessed with time—
precious moments of the day—
lost in the counting—

## WILD SALT BURNING

I remember the taste of the salt wind
The streaming night so black in your hair
Sweet jasmine in the courtyard
Breathing a prayer

*And the moon drown in your eyes*
*And the great wheel turning*
*And the deep song calling us*
*Wild salt burning*

I remember your touch as you came to me
My body on fire—my heart beating
The slow and lovely closeness of you
Our lips meeting

*And the moon drown in your eyes*
*And the great wheel turning*
*And the deep song calling us*
*Wild salt burning*

# PIAF
*For Piaf and Dr Graham Futter*


She lay on some old newspaper
in the gutter of Concert Boulevard

I stopped the car

She was alive

I took off my jacket and wrapped her in it
She did not resist

At the vet he examined her
She was skin and bone with a few tufts of hair

Will we have to put her down, I asked

He held her up to look at her

She turned to face him
Cocked her head—

I waited

No, he said
She has managed so far
Let's give her a chance

So we did

I have a photograph of her next to me
as I write
running in the wind

a black husky with a white face
white legs and white-tipped tail

unforgettable

# TOUCH

this could well be the place
but you are not ready for it

so do not return to it another day
for it will not allow you back a second time

and do not consult the hourglass
with its slow
and silent
fall
of sand

for with every grain
it will erase all the beauty you have dreamed
and fling it far from you
and your longing with it

and do not think to possess it
nor even the thought of it—held in the mind
—for it can fly—
where no mind can go

but somewhere—
beyond wonder—
within a holy emptiness
—and beautiful beyond imagination—
there is an infinitely sad and sacred touch—that calls to you
—has always called—

it was always with you
—One Breath—

## LOOK FOR ME
*for Jacques*

Look for me in wild places
—always close to water—
That's all she said—


## I AND THOU

you are a quiet voice of pain
a full and gentle tide in me
whose rhythmic surge and ebb conjoin
my own pulse throbbing—

you are a sweetness I have drunk
and a strange loving
which is so much a part of me
and growing—

## I AM THOU

I am—Thou
through all the nights and days of time
and beyond all time
and even as a Spirit Wind
I am

## HAIKU

Now—in the nowhere—
and—now—feeling the no-thing
blowing through my soul—

# Saint Francis Veterinary Hospital, Cape Town

For just short of four decades, I have been taking a variety of canine kin to Saint Francis for a wide array of treatments.

During this time wonderful vets, hospital nurses, kennelmen, grooming specialists, puppy trainers and welcoming desk and information assistants have come and gone.

To all of you, wherever you are now, I and an array of canine family members say a huge thank you for all your incredible, loving attention and skilful service.

To those of you who presently fill those positions, many of whom I have known for years now, it is always such a pleasure to be welcomed by you. You have become a second, and extremely important family to us.

But there is one person who, throughout all of these arrivals and departures, has remained a constant, stalwart presence—I might say the beacon of stability for Saint Francis: Dr Graham Futter.

We were both somewhere in our early forties when I first crossed the threshold, sometime in the 1980s, after our family moved house. There are very few people that I have seen for that period of time, so regularly and so consistently, as Graham, because of my visits to Saint Francis. During this time, dogs and puppies have happily arrived, and sadly departed, having received attention for the array of needs that present themselves over a canine lifetime. It has been a comforting and reliable port of call through many a crisis. What I associate with all of these visits are: skilled medical practice, friendship, warmth and compassion.

Over these latter years—maybe two decades—it has been to Graham that I have turned most often; possibly because my dogs' needs and mine could not be quite so separately defined. Perhaps it requires an older person to read and appreciate an ageing dog-owner's needs more accurately, and how this might impact on and become part of ongoing management suggestions and treatment for the canine patient.

Now my last two beloved dogs have died, within a few months of each other. I will not be looking for others. It is the end of an essential part of my life, so filled with joy, and canine humour—a rich and humbling experience of unconditional love, and all that it teaches us.

Cracker, my husband's guide dog, also ageing, lives with us now. He attends a different vet practice.
I may have to become an eccentric non-dog-owner, who pops into Saint Francis from time to time to buy dog toys and treats, and the occasional bag of dog food—for Tears (The Emma Animal Rescue Society). Some habits are hard to break.

Graham—thank you, from the bottom of our human and canine hearts, for all that you have ever done for us.
Thank you, most importantly, for all that you are.

With love and gratitude—

Barbara

## ACKNOWLEDGEMENTS

The following poems were first published as a collection in *The Love Sheet: Barbara Fairhead & Jacques Coetzee* by Hands-On Books in 2017:

Song for the Duende
Casa Milagro
Leaving the world
The Matrix
Howl
A New Voice
Late Summer
The Road Heads East
The River Beneath the River
Tokai
Stone Cottage—West Coast
Ode to Mystery

The following poems were first published in *Stanzas* Issue 19: May 2020:
Naked
Soul
Imprint

'Full-moon Vigil' was first published in *Heart of Africa!* African Sun Press 2014, selected by Patricia Schonstein.

My grateful thanks go to the following people for all their help and wonderful encouragement during the compilation of this book:

Jo Ractliffe: for the cover photograph: Muizenberg, 1987.

Trilby Krepelka: for making the format changes for the final book dimensions; for being the essential, and exhaustive 'go-between' in the many discussions regarding the logistics of getting the book printed.

Sherry Woods: for setting up the essential, original format, and for her attention to detail during periodic check-ups.

Arja Salafranca: for editing this large manuscript; for her keen attention to detail and her diplomatic patience.

Colleen Higgs: my publisher at Hands-On Books, for all the extra help she offered so willingly to bring this book to completion.

Jacques Coetzee: my husband, for all his constant encouragement, his wise, and informed suggestions, and his hawk-eye editing.

Finally, I want to acknowledge and bless all the many Faces of Kin, that have been such a rich part of my life.